# The Patented Works of J. Hutton Pulitzer

METHOD OF CONTROLLING A COMPUTER USING
AN EMBEDDED UNIQUE CODE IN THE CONTENT OF
DVD MEDIA

*Patent Number: 7,010,577*
*Date of Patent: March 7, 2006*

# A Contradiction in Time

In 1985, leaving the comfortable world of a Fortune 500 company to pursue my own entrepreneurial dreams/venture was a mutually terrifying and electrifying proposition.

At that time, comfort for me was defined as "Corporate America". And my mega-corporation world included over twenty-five years spent in Senior Executive positions with AT&T, General Electric, Oracle and British Telecom.

But in 1985 I took that "leap of faith" and purchased a company whereby I could pursue my entrepreneurial dreams. In doing so, I inherited a young employee associated with that company who I immediately recognized had great potential. He was smart, quick to learn and searching for knowledge to become a powerful and influential force in both the business world and society (his career had just begun). He left an indelible impression on me, one that has been branded in my mind for over thirty years (as I write this prologue).

This initial venture in 1985 was my first into the mostly solo activities associated with the entrepreneurial world. In the 80's becoming an Entrepreneur was the "New-New". Most seasoned executives in Corporate America wanted to become one, and all had taken full notice of the ultimate entrepreneur – STEVE JOBS – as the dynamic entrepreneur who could build a huge company, and yet still move and be as nimble as a newly minted entrepreneur.

During this time, all seasoned executives were "*In Search of Excellence*" (by Tom Peters). Dreams were big and visionaries were leading the way; but few either had the nerve or possessed the willing to take the risk outside of the corporate world to be a true entrepreneur.

With that first acquisition of a small company came one individual, which would change my life in many ways. Funny, to even type that since I was the seasoned Fortune 500 Executive who was going to teach him the ways of the corporate world and this person was just barely out of his teens.

From the day, as the new company owner and meeting him, my soul knew he would accomplish great things. Great things, maybe not in the traditional orthodox manner that most people understand/expect, but in a manner that is unique to HIS way of achieving his goals for mankind. I trusted my natural instincts then and he has proven them right to this day.

Just as with any business, time marches on and things change and within a few years this young visionary left my tutelage to forge his own entrepreneurial path. Coming from the mega corporation's culture and now eighteen years as an

entrepreneur, I have had the opportunity to work with extremely talented individuals, but none can match the creative mind/talents of J. Hutton Pulitzer.

Pulitzer is the ultimate contradiction if they're ever was one. The duality of what he was and could be is amazing. On one hand an incredible presenter and salesman, while on the other a loner/society recluse. An incredible technical genius that does not write a lick of code, a maniacal visionary who often runs and thinks too fast for the average person, but yet continually alters his activities to help others to understand and/or succeed; but yet probably cares too much about what people think at times.

Truly a contradiction:

Like Steve Jobs, Pulitzer's mind thinks and works differently when it comes to life and impacting society in multiple ways. One of his most cherished achievements was the development and implementation of the world's first "global positioning system for the Internet" (i.e. the CueCat™). Definitely ahead of the times, Pulitzer's vision for accessing the Internet in a unique manner was sponsored and financed by such corporate giants as RadioShack, ING Barings, Coca-Cola, NBC, etc. for a total of $200 million and successful individuals such as Steven Spielberg, Steve Forbes, etc. Top manufacturers and corporations throughout the world understood and invested in the :CRQ Cue Code technology because they shared Pulitzer's vision and knew it would "bridge the gap" between consumers and their companies. But consumers were slow to "understand" the new technology and the Internet market crash in 2000-2001 ended the rapid success of his company's (Digital Convergence, Inc.) technology in its initial form; but yet still today, over two billion consumers around the world a day utilize some derivative of his initial patents.

Nevertheless, Pulitzer's patents and his creative visions continue to thrive in today's highly complex and technological environment. Even today, when you board an American Airlines flight, the boarding agent utilizes a derivative of Pulitzer's scanning patent when he/she scans your Boarding Pass for the flight. And Smart Phones of all types/manufacturers utilize the patented technology that Pulitzer originally invented with his Chief Technology Officer at Digital Convergence in the late 1990's.

Bottom line, society should not dismiss or misjudge Pulitzer in the future. Other entrepreneurs like him who themselves have failed several times in their careers have proven to be geniuses when their total careers are evaluated. Pulitzer is the ultimate Type "A" personality and he continues to think creatively and decisively, which in time will certainly impact our lives again...... I can guarantee this!

To this day, more than 30 years later, we still work together. It is certainly a challenge to work beside him but I feel honored to be his co-worker and friend. Today our roles have changed and I am learning from him. To understand him is

As a trusted and extraordinary individual, J. Hutton Pulitzer has continually demonstrated a unique ability to see ahead in time and forecast the future with an uncanny degree of accuracy. Many times over the past 32 years that I have known him, he has creatively and successfully leveraged his visions of the future in order to insure the success of many types of business ventures.

Having experienced the agony of competitive inroads associated with some of his early projects, Hutton quickly studied all aspects surrounding the sophisticated art of drafting patents and has "mastered" the ability to author and construct patents in a manner that are "iron clad" in blocking competitive inroads by outside entities. His effectiveness can be substantiated via his present patent portfolio, which includes global patents granted in 189 countries (a feat most inventors never attain).

His unique and personal approach in constructing patents has proven to be extremely successful which is further substantiated by his single best unmatched patent ratio of forty-nine citations per one patent (i.e. 49:1 ratio) and the fact that he currently holds an unparalleled patent granted record of 98.8%.

In addition to authoring unique and complex patents, he is extremely experienced in the art of constructing original patents in such a manner as to anticipate future potential infringements associated with any/all patents he writes. Hutton takes a multi-dimensional view of possible competitive inroads, as well as, the anticipation of the creative and unique ways in which his patents can be implemented. Thereby, re-enforcing the protection armor in which he builds into each and every patent he develops.

Bottom-line, his patent expertise routinely exceeds his client's and/or the industry's expectations; while effectively insuring each and every patent he develops in such a manner as to prevent any potential work around and/or patent penetration in future years. As a result, patent experts from around the world routinely keep a keen eye on Mr. Pulitzer's patent work and filings in order to possibly anticipate his vision and actions regarding the future.

As the result of Pulitzer's developing an industry around connecting codes where one did not exist before, he became the "Father" of what is now known as "Scan-To-Connect" and "Scan Commerce". Two brand new features Hutton bestowed upon the Internet in the late 90's.

But with every new industry and technology comes competition and jealously; therefore I will quote one Billionaire's comment about Pulitzer's idea for bar codes to connect to the Internet via scanning:

### *"The stupidest invention ever!"*

That quote, which was carried by numerous newspapers, magazines and blogs when uttered was like the shot heard around the world at the time the dot com industry was crashing in 2000-2001.

But like Steve Jobs, Pulitzer is a patient man and visionaries do NOT let their dreams die. Pulitzer implemented his vision and pursued his patents for "Scan to Commerce" and "Scan to Connect" and as I mentioned above, today over two billion people around the world utilize a derivative of his original scanning patents on a daily basis. ***A multibillion-dollar industry created from the vision of a "contradiction in time".***

I say, in closing *"Two Billion daily users of his technology a day! Not bad for the stupidest invention ever!"*

***Can't wait to see his next stupid idea***!

**Blaine L. Thacker**, Ex-Corporate Executive & Entrepreneur

P.S. You should view the movie "JOBS" (i.e. Steve Jobs) to truly understand and appreciate J. Hutton Pulitzer.

US007010577B1

(12) **United States Patent**  (10) **Patent No.:** **US 7,010,577 B1**
Philyaw et al.  (45) **Date of Patent:** *Mar. 7, 2006

(54) **METHOD OF CONTROLLING A COMPUTER USING AN EMBEDDED UNIQUE CODE IN THE CONTENT OF DVD MEDIA**

(75) Inventors: **Jeffry Jovan Philyaw**, Dallas, TX (US); **David Kent Mathews**, Carrollton, TX (US)

(73) Assignee: **L. V. Partners, L.P.**, Dallas, TX (US)

( * ) Notice: Subject to any disclaimer, the term of this patent is extended or adjusted under 35 U.S.C. 154(b) by 0 days.

This patent is subject to a terminal disclaimer.

(21) Appl. No.: **09/378,218**

(22) Filed: **Aug. 19, 1999**

**Related U.S. Application Data**

(63) Continuation-in-part of application No. 09/151,530, filed on Sep. 11, 1998, now Pat. No. 6,098,106.

(51) **Int. Cl.**
*G06F 15/16* (2006.01)
(52) **U.S. Cl.** ..................................... **709/217**; 709/238
(58) **Field of Classification Search** ............... 709/238, 709/239, 240, 241, 242, 245, 217, 218, 226, 709/219; 386/125, 126; 725/135, 136, 34
See application file for complete search history.

(56) **References Cited**

U.S. PATENT DOCUMENTS

| | | | |
|---|---|---|---|
| 3,668,312 A | 6/1972 | Yamamoto et al. | .......... 178/6.8 |
| 4,002,886 A | 1/1977 | Sundelin | ................ 235/61.7 R |
| 4,042,792 A | 8/1977 | Pakenham et al. | ............ 179/90 |
| 4,365,148 A | 12/1982 | Whitney | ..................... 235/383 |
| 4,621,259 A | 11/1986 | Schepers et al. | ............ 340/707 |
| 4,654,482 A | 3/1987 | DeAngelis | ................... 379/95 |
| 4,780,599 A | 10/1988 | Baus | .......................... 235/383 |
| 4,785,296 A | 11/1988 | Tabata et al. | ............... 340/731 |
| 4,816,904 A | 3/1989 | McKenna et al. | ............ 358/84 |

| | | | |
|---|---|---|---|
| 4,817,136 A | 3/1989 | Rhoads | ....................... 379/357 |

(Continued)

FOREIGN PATENT DOCUMENTS

EP 0 961 250 A2 12/1999

(Continued)

OTHER PUBLICATIONS

"Group Decision Support System: Development and Application", Energy Systems, Westinghouse, Pittsburgh, PA.

(Continued)

*Primary Examiner*—Marc D. Thompson
(74) *Attorney, Agent, or Firm*—Howison & Arnott, L.L.P.

(57) **ABSTRACT**

A method for allowing a user PC to be controlled in order to effect a connection between the user PC and a destination node on a network. This is facilitated through an audio source wherein the content of digital video disk recording media has embedded therein an audio signal. When the recording media is played, the audio signal is extracted by an audio extractor and transmitted to the user PC, and detected by a program running in the background of the user PC. Once the audible tone is detected, a web browser is launched and the tone or decoded product identifier information associated with the tone is transmitted to an ARS on the network. The ARS then compares the information received from the user PC using information from a relational database. The relational database contains routing information for various destination nodes on the network. When a match occurs, the matching information is then forwarded back to the user PC and this is utilized to route the user PC to the particular destination node corresponding to the audible tone for the processing of information received therefrom.

**6 Claims, 8 Drawing Sheets**

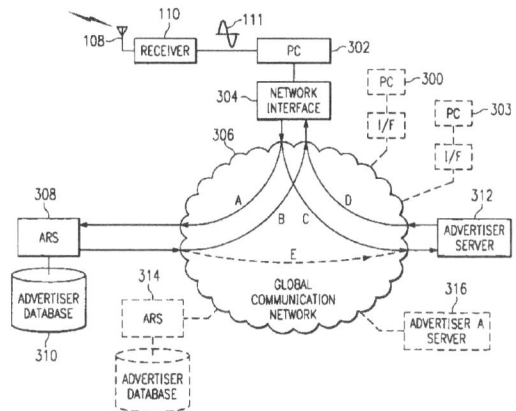

## U.S. PATENT DOCUMENTS

| | | | |
|---|---|---|---|
| 4,833,308 A | 5/1989 | Humble | 235/383 |
| 4,841,132 A | 6/1989 | Kajitani et al. | 235/472 |
| 4,845,634 A | 7/1989 | Vitek et al. | 364/468 |
| 4,894,789 A | 1/1990 | Yee | 364/521 |
| 4,899,370 A | 2/1990 | Kameo et al. | 379/104 |
| 4,901,073 A | 2/1990 | Kibrick | 341/13 |
| 4,905,094 A | 2/1990 | Pocock et al. | 358/342 |
| 4,907,264 A | 3/1990 | Seiler et al. | 379/355 |
| 4,916,293 A | 4/1990 | Cartlidge et al. | 235/375 |
| 4,937,853 A | 6/1990 | Brule et al. | 379/96 |
| 4,947,028 A | 8/1990 | Gorog | 235/381 |
| 4,959,530 A | 9/1990 | O'Connor | 235/383 |
| 4,975,948 A | 12/1990 | Andresen et al. | 379/355 |
| 4,984,155 A | 1/1991 | Geier et al. | 364/401 |
| 5,038,023 A | 8/1991 | Saliga | 235/385 |
| 5,054,096 A | 10/1991 | Beizer | 382/41 |
| 5,088,045 A | 2/1992 | Shimanaka et al. | 364/468 |
| 5,111,391 A | 5/1992 | Fields et al. | 364/401 |
| 5,115,326 A | 5/1992 | Burgess et al. | 358/440 |
| 5,128,752 A | 7/1992 | Von Kohorn | 358/84 |
| 5,144,654 A | 9/1992 | Kelley et al. | 379/356 |
| 5,161,037 A | 11/1992 | Saito | 358/468 |
| 5,161,214 A | 11/1992 | Addink et al. | 395/145 |
| 5,182,705 A | 1/1993 | Barr et al. | 364/401 |
| 5,189,630 A | 2/1993 | Barstow et al. | 364/514 |
| 5,191,525 A | 3/1993 | LeBrun et al. | 364/419 |
| 5,198,644 A | 3/1993 | Pfeiffer et al. | 235/383 |
| 5,213,337 A * | 5/1993 | Sherman | 725/136 |
| 5,235,654 A | 8/1993 | Anderson et al. | 382/61 |
| 5,241,402 A | 8/1993 | Aboujaoude et al. | 358/406 |
| 5,243,531 A | 9/1993 | DiPippo et al. | 364/468 |
| 5,247,347 A | 9/1993 | Litteral et al. | 358/85 |
| 5,247,697 A * | 9/1993 | Ban | 709/245 |
| 5,262,860 A | 11/1993 | Fitzpatrick et al. | 358/142 |
| 5,285,278 A | 2/1994 | Holman | 358/142 |
| 5,287,181 A | 2/1994 | Holman | 348/473 |
| 5,288,976 A | 2/1994 | Citron et al. | 235/375 |
| 5,296,688 A | 3/1994 | Hamilton et al. | 235/375 |
| 5,304,786 A | 4/1994 | Pavlidis et al. | 235/462 |
| 5,305,195 A | 4/1994 | Murphy | 364/401 |
| 5,319,454 A | 6/1994 | Schutte | 348/5.5 |
| 5,324,922 A | 6/1994 | Roberts | 235/375 |
| 5,331,547 A | 7/1994 | Laszlo | 364/413.01 |
| 5,340,966 A | 8/1994 | Morimoto | 235/376 |
| 5,357,276 A | 10/1994 | Banker et al. | 348/7 |
| 5,362,948 A | 11/1994 | Morimoto | 235/376 |
| 5,382,779 A | 1/1995 | Gupta | 235/383 |
| 5,386,298 A | 1/1995 | Bronnenberg et al. | 358/403 |
| 5,398,336 A | 3/1995 | Tantry et al. | 395/600 |
| 5,405,232 A | 4/1995 | Lloyd et al. | 414/280 |
| 5,418,713 A | 5/1995 | Allen | 364/403 |
| 5,420,403 A | 5/1995 | Allum et al. | 235/375 |
| 5,420,943 A | 5/1995 | Mak | 382/313 |
| 5,424,524 A | 6/1995 | Ruppert et al. | 235/462 |
| 5,438,355 A | 8/1995 | Palmer | 348/1 |
| 5,446,490 A | 8/1995 | Blahut et al. | 348/7 |
| 5,446,919 A | 8/1995 | Wilkins | 455/6.2 |
| 5,491,508 A | 2/1996 | Friedell et al. | 348/16 |
| 5,493,107 A | 2/1996 | Gupta et al. | 235/383 |
| 5,519,878 A | 5/1996 | Dolin, Jr. | 395/800 |
| 5,530,852 A | 6/1996 | Meske, Jr. et al. | 396/600 |
| 5,570,295 A | 10/1996 | Isenberg et al. | 364/514 |
| 5,572,643 A | 11/1996 | Judson | 395/793 |
| 5,592,551 A | 1/1997 | Lett et al. | 380/20 |
| 5,594,226 A | 1/1997 | Steger | 235/379 |
| 5,602,377 A | 2/1997 | Beller et al. | 235/462 |
| 5,604,542 A | 2/1997 | Dedrick | 348/552 |
| 5,640,193 A | 6/1997 | Wellner | 348/7 |
| 5,649,186 A | 7/1997 | Ferguson | 395/610 |
| 5,664,110 A | 9/1997 | Green et al. | 705/26 |
| 5,671,226 A * | 9/1997 | Murakami et al. | |
| 5,671,282 A | 9/1997 | Wolff et al. | 380/25 |
| 5,675,721 A | 10/1997 | Freedman et al. | 395/129 |
| 5,682,540 A | 10/1997 | Klotz, Jr. et al. | 395/766 |
| 5,694,163 A | 12/1997 | Harrison | 348/13 |
| 5,708,780 A | 1/1998 | Levergood et al. | 395/200.12 |
| 5,710,887 A | 1/1998 | Chelliah et al. | 395/226 |
| 5,715,314 A | 2/1998 | Payne et al. | 380/24 |
| 5,724,424 A | 3/1998 | Gifford | 380/24 |
| 5,740,369 A * | 4/1998 | Yokozawa et al. | 709/217 |
| 5,745,681 A | 4/1998 | Levine et al. | 395/200.3 |
| 5,754,906 A | 5/1998 | Yoshida | 396/448 |
| 5,757,917 A | 5/1998 | Rose et al. | 380/25 |
| 5,761,606 A | 6/1998 | Wolzien | 455/6.2 |
| 5,764,906 A | 6/1998 | Edelstein et al. | 395/200.49 |
| 5,765,176 A | 6/1998 | Bloomberg | 707/514 |
| 5,768,528 A | 6/1998 | Stumm | 395/200.61 |
| 5,774,660 A * | 6/1998 | Brendel et al. | 709/239 |
| 5,774,664 A | 6/1998 | Hidary et al. | 395/200 |
| 5,774,666 A * | 6/1998 | Portuesi | 725/131 |
| 5,774,870 A | 6/1998 | Storey | 705/14 |
| 5,778,367 A | 7/1998 | Wesinger, Jr. et al. | 707/10 |
| 5,790,793 A | 8/1998 | Higley | 395/200.48 |
| 5,791,991 A | 8/1998 | Small | 463/41 |
| 5,794,210 A | 8/1998 | Goldhaber et al. | 705/14 |
| 5,796,952 A | 8/1998 | Davis et al. | 305/200.54 |
| 5,804,803 A | 9/1998 | Cragun et al. | 235/375 |
| 5,815,776 A | 9/1998 | Nukada | 399/174 |
| 5,832,223 A | 11/1998 | Hara et al. | 395/200.47 |
| 5,833,468 A | 11/1998 | Guy et al. | 434/350 |
| 5,848,202 A | 12/1998 | D'Eri et al. | 382/306 |
| 5,848,413 A | 12/1998 | Wolff | 707/10 |
| 5,854,897 A | 12/1998 | Radziewicz et al. | 709/224 |
| 5,864,823 A | 1/1999 | Levitan | 105/14 |
| 5,869,819 A | 2/1999 | Knowles et al. | 235/375 |
| 5,905,248 A | 5/1999 | Russell et al. | 235/462 |
| 5,905,251 A | 5/1999 | Knowles | 235/472.01 |
| 5,905,665 A | 5/1999 | Rim | 364/746 |
| 5,905,865 A | 5/1999 | Palmer et al. | 395/200.47 |
| 5,907,793 A | 5/1999 | Reams | 455/3.1 |
| 5,913,210 A | 6/1999 | Call | 707/4 |
| 5,915,090 A | 6/1999 | Joseph et al. | 709/202 |
| 5,918,214 A | 6/1999 | Perkowski | 705/27 |
| 5,925,865 A | 7/1999 | Steger | 235/379 |
| 5,929,850 A | 7/1999 | Broadwin et al. | 345/327 |
| 5,932,863 A | 8/1999 | Rathus et al. | 235/462.15 |
| 5,933,829 A | 8/1999 | Durst et al. | 707/10 |
| 5,937,163 A * | 8/1999 | Lee et al. | 709/218 |
| 5,937,164 A * | 8/1999 | Mages et al. | 709/218 |
| 5,948,061 A | 9/1999 | Merriman et al. | 709/219 |
| 5,957,695 A | 9/1999 | Redford et al. | 434/307 R |
| 5,960,411 A | 9/1999 | Hartman et al. | 705/26 |
| 5,961,603 A | 10/1999 | Kunkel et al. | 709/229 |
| 5,970,471 A | 10/1999 | Hill | 705/26 |
| 5,970,472 A | 10/1999 | Allsop et al. | 705/26 |
| 5,971,277 A | 10/1999 | Cragun et al. | 235/462.01 |
| 5,974,443 A | 10/1999 | Jeske | 709/202 |
| 5,974,451 A | 10/1999 | Simmons | 709/218 |
| 5,976,833 A | 11/1999 | Furukawa et al. | 435/69.1 |
| 5,978,773 A * | 11/1999 | Hudetz et al. | 709/219 |
| 5,991,739 A | 11/1999 | Cupps et al. | 705/26 |
| 5,992,752 A | 11/1999 | Wilz, Sr. et al. | 235/472.01 |
| 5,995,105 A | 11/1999 | Reber et al. | 345/356 |
| 6,002,394 A | 12/1999 | Schein et al. | 345/327 |
| 6,003,073 A | 12/1999 | Solvason | 709/219 |
| 6,006,257 A | 12/1999 | Slezak | 709/219 |
| 6,009,410 A | 12/1999 | LeMole et al. | 709/219 |
| 6,009,465 A | 12/1999 | Decker et al. | 709/219 |
| 6,012,102 A | 1/2000 | Shachar | 710/5 |
| 6,014,701 A * | 1/2000 | Chaddha | 709/226 |
| 6,018,764 A | 1/2000 | Field et al. | 709/217 |
| 6,018,768 A * | 1/2000 | Ullman et al. | 709/218 |
| 6,049,539 A | 4/2000 | Lee et al. | 370/355 |
| 6,061,368 A * | 5/2000 | Hitzelberger | 709/238 |

| | | | | |
|---|---|---|---|---|
| 6,061,719 A | * | 5/2000 | Bendinelli et al. | 709/218 |
| 6,064,979 A | | 5/2000 | Perkowski | 705/26 |
| 6,108,656 A | | 8/2000 | Durst et al. | 707/10 |
| 6,195,693 B1 | | 2/2001 | Berry et al. | |
| 6,400,407 B1 | * | 6/2002 | Zigmond et al. | 725/51 |
| 6,580,870 B1 | * | 6/2003 | Kanazawa et al. | 386/95 |

### FOREIGN PATENT DOCUMENTS

| | | |
|---|---|---|
| JP | 10188140 A | 12/1996 |
| WO | WO 95/10813 | 10/1994 |
| WO | WO 96/07146 | 9/1995 |
| WO | WO 97/37319 | 2/1997 |
| WO | WO 98/09243 | 8/1997 |
| WO | WO 98/03923 | 1/1998 |
| WO | WO 98/06055 | 2/1998 |
| WO | WO 98/19259 | 5/1998 |
| WO | WO 98/40823 | 9/1998 |
| WO | WO 99/63457 | 6/1999 |

### OTHER PUBLICATIONS

"New Technologies in Credit Card Authentication", Pieter de Bryne, Institute for Communications Technology, Zurich, Switzerland.

"AVITAL, a Private Teaching System by Fax Communication", Atsusji Iizawa, Noriro Sugiki, Yukari Shitora and Hideko Kunii, Software Research Center, Tokyo, Japan.

"Document on Computer" USPS Technical Support Center, Norman, OK.

"Development of a Commercially Successful Wearable Data Collection System", Symbol Technologies, Inc.

What do forward looking companies consider in their plans and developements?, A.G. Johnston, Nestle.

"The Automation Synergy", Neves and Noivo, Portugal.

"Integration of Hand-Written Address Interpretation Technology into the United States Postal Service Remote Computer Reader System", Srihari (Cedar, Suny at Buffalo) and Kueberg (U.S. Postal Services, VA).

"Paper Based Document Security—A Review", van Renesse, TNO Institute of Applied Physics, The Netherlands.

"IEEE Standard for Bar Coding for Distribution Transformers" Transformers Committee of the IEEE Power Engineering Society, The Institute of Electrical and Electronics Engineers, Inc. NY.

"The Stylus™-Shopping from Home", STYLUS Innovation, MA.

"Distributing Uniform Resource Locators as Bar Code Images", IBM Technical Disclosure Bulleting, Jan. 1996.

"Bar Code Method for Automating Catalog Orders", IBM Technical Disclosure Bulletin, Sep. 1998.

"Bar Code Recognition System Using Image Processing", Kuroki, Yoncoka et al., Hitachi Research Laborator.

* cited by examiner

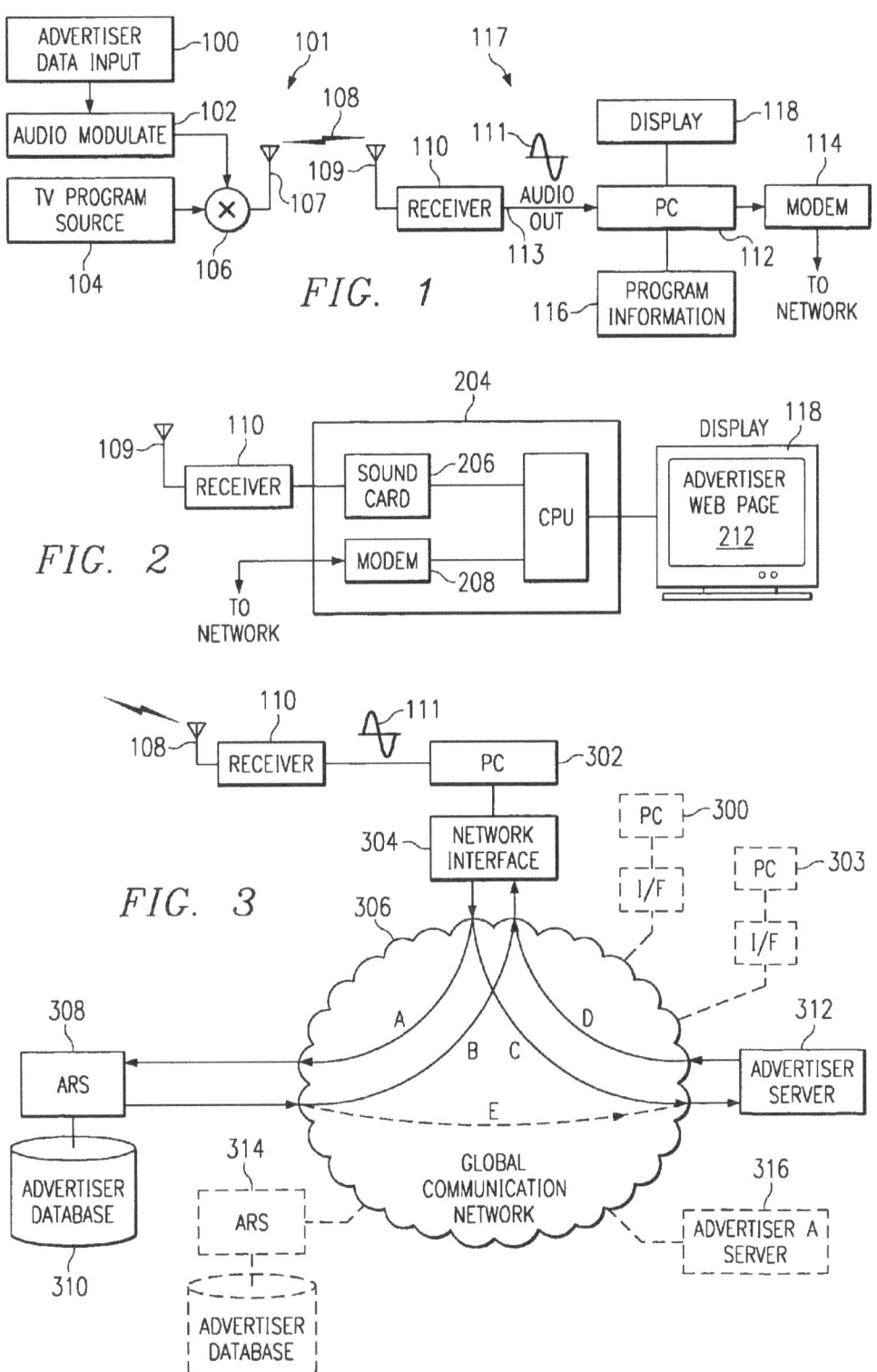

FIG. 1

FIG. 2

FIG. 3

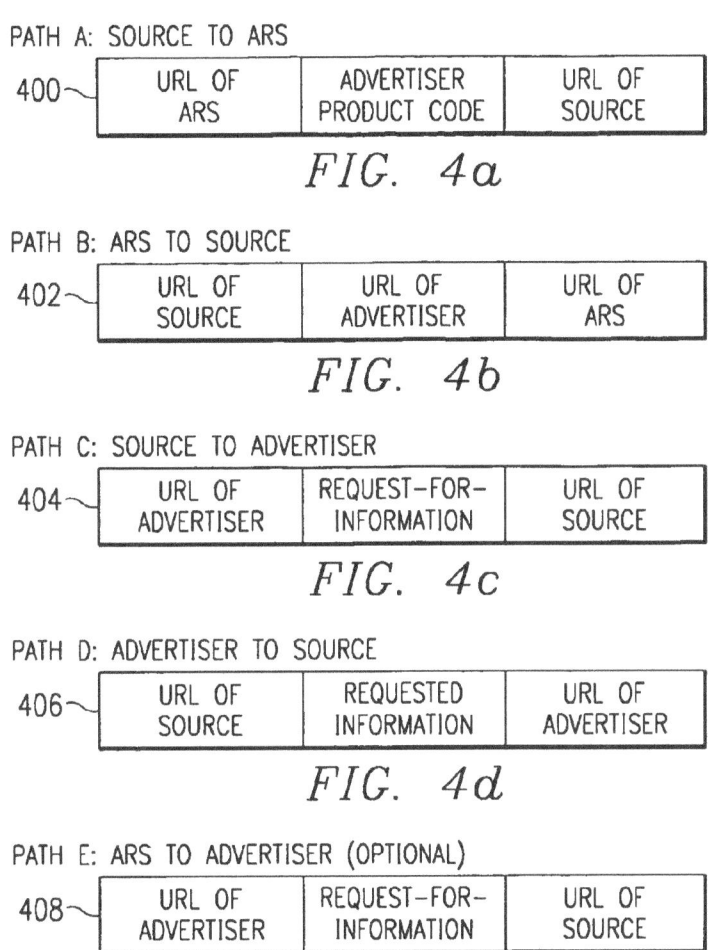

PATH A: SOURCE TO ARS

| URL OF ARS | ADVERTISER PRODUCT CODE | URL OF SOURCE |

400

*FIG. 4a*

PATH B: ARS TO SOURCE

| URL OF SOURCE | URL OF ADVERTISER | URL OF ARS |

402

*FIG. 4b*

PATH C: SOURCE TO ADVERTISER

| URL OF ADVERTISER | REQUEST-FOR-INFORMATION | URL OF SOURCE |

404

*FIG. 4c*

PATH D: ADVERTISER TO SOURCE

| URL OF SOURCE | REQUESTED INFORMATION | URL OF ADVERTISER |

406

*FIG. 4d*

PATH E: ARS TO ADVERTISER (OPTIONAL)

| URL OF ADVERTISER | REQUEST-FOR-INFORMATION | URL OF SOURCE |

408

*FIG. 4e*

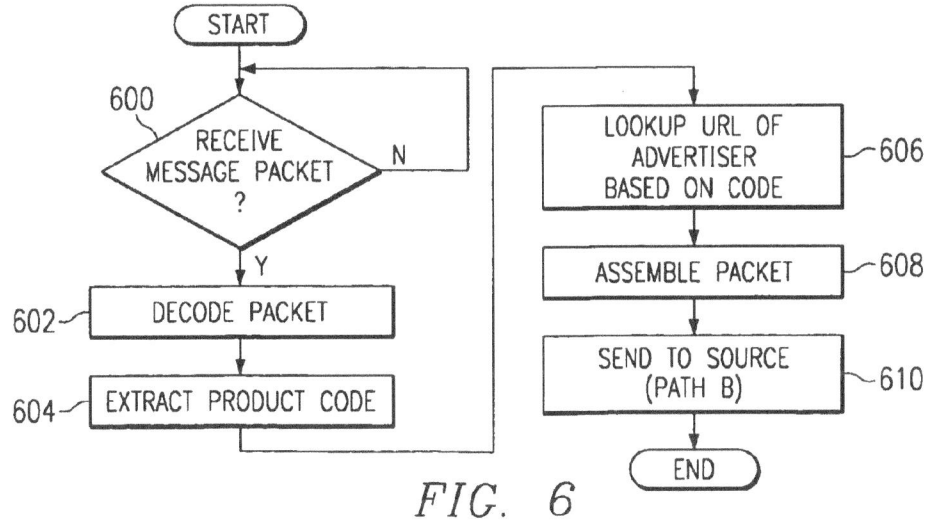

*FIG. 6*

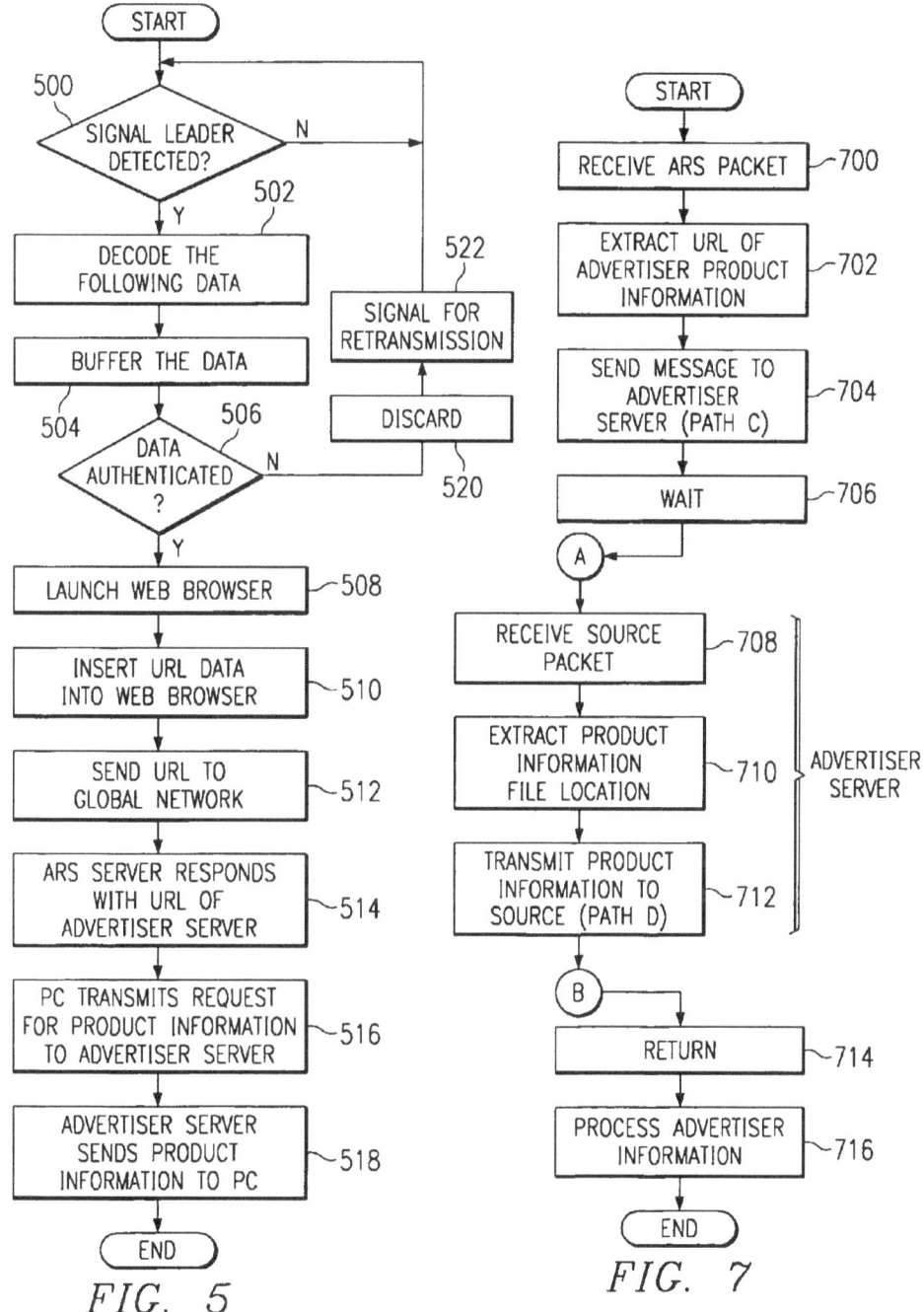

FIG. 5

FIG. 7

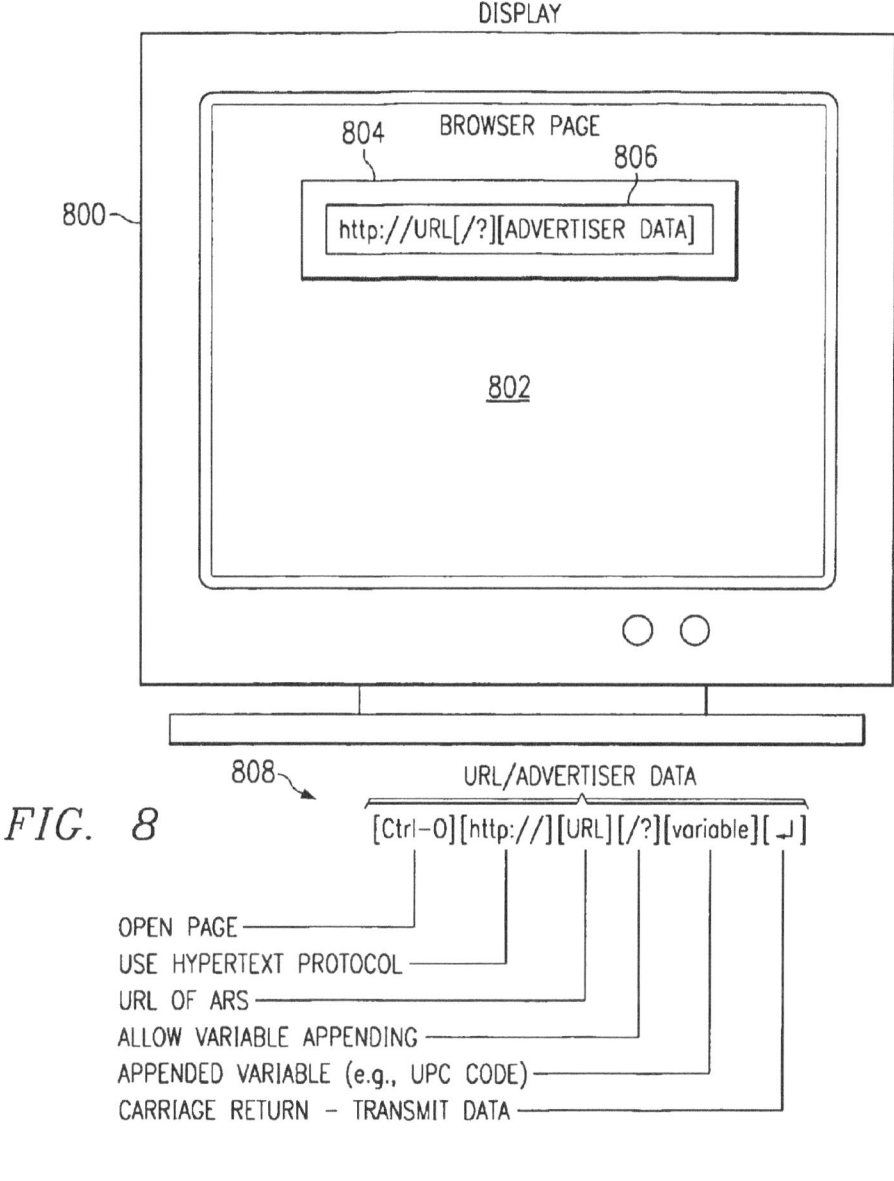

DISPLAY

BROWSER PAGE

804

806

http://URL[/?][ADVERTISER DATA]

800

802

URL/ADVERTISER DATA

808

FIG. 8

[Ctrl-O][http://][URL][/?][variable][↵]

OPEN PAGE
USE HYPERTEXT PROTOCOL
URL OF ARS
ALLOW VARIABLE APPENDING
APPENDED VARIABLE (e.g., UPC CODE)
CARRIAGE RETURN – TRANSMIT DATA

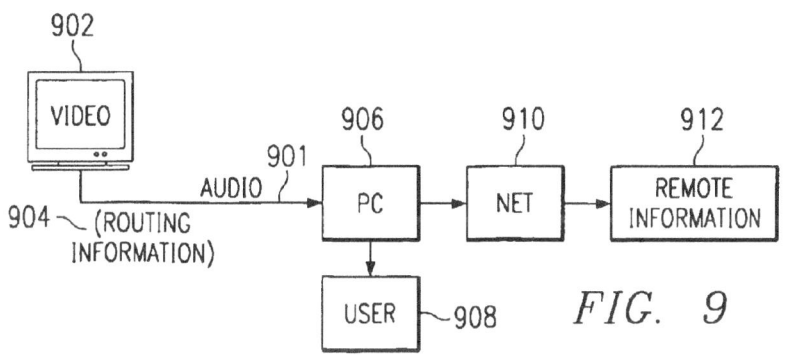

902

VIDEO

906    910    912

901

AUDIO

904 (ROUTING INFORMATION)

PC    NET    REMOTE INFORMATION

USER 908

FIG. 9

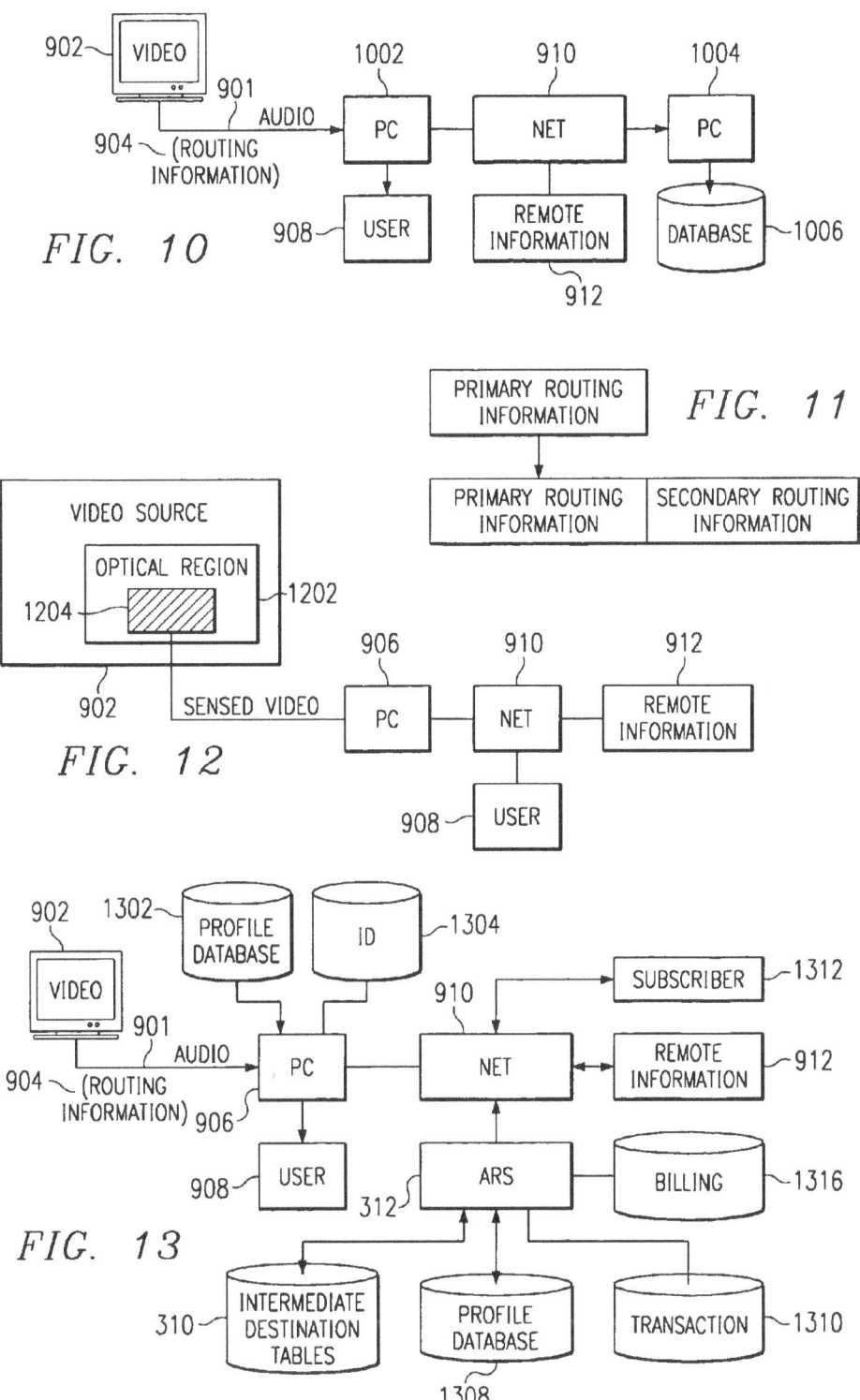

FIG. 10

FIG. 11

FIG. 12

FIG. 13

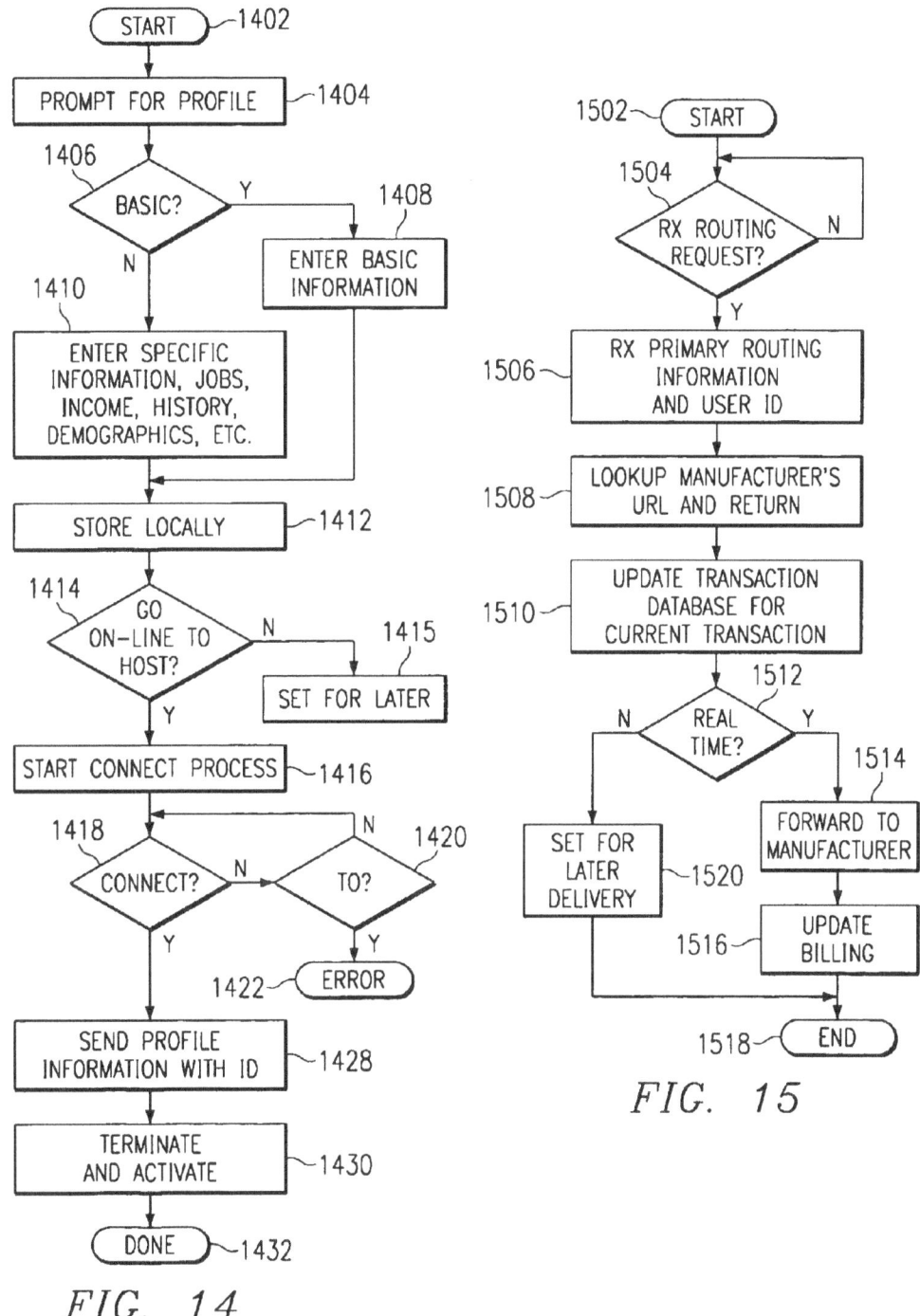

FIG. 14

FIG. 15

*FIG. 16*

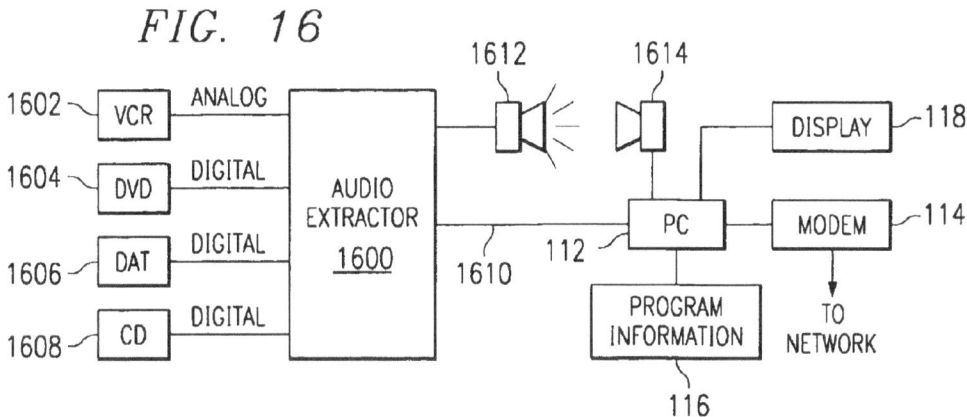

*FIG. 17*

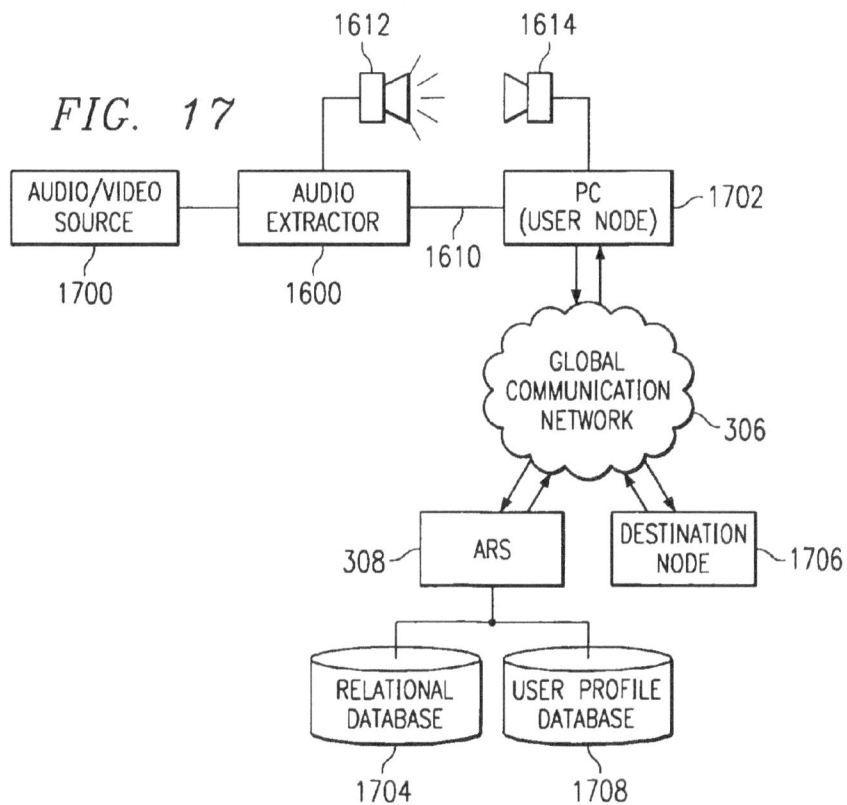

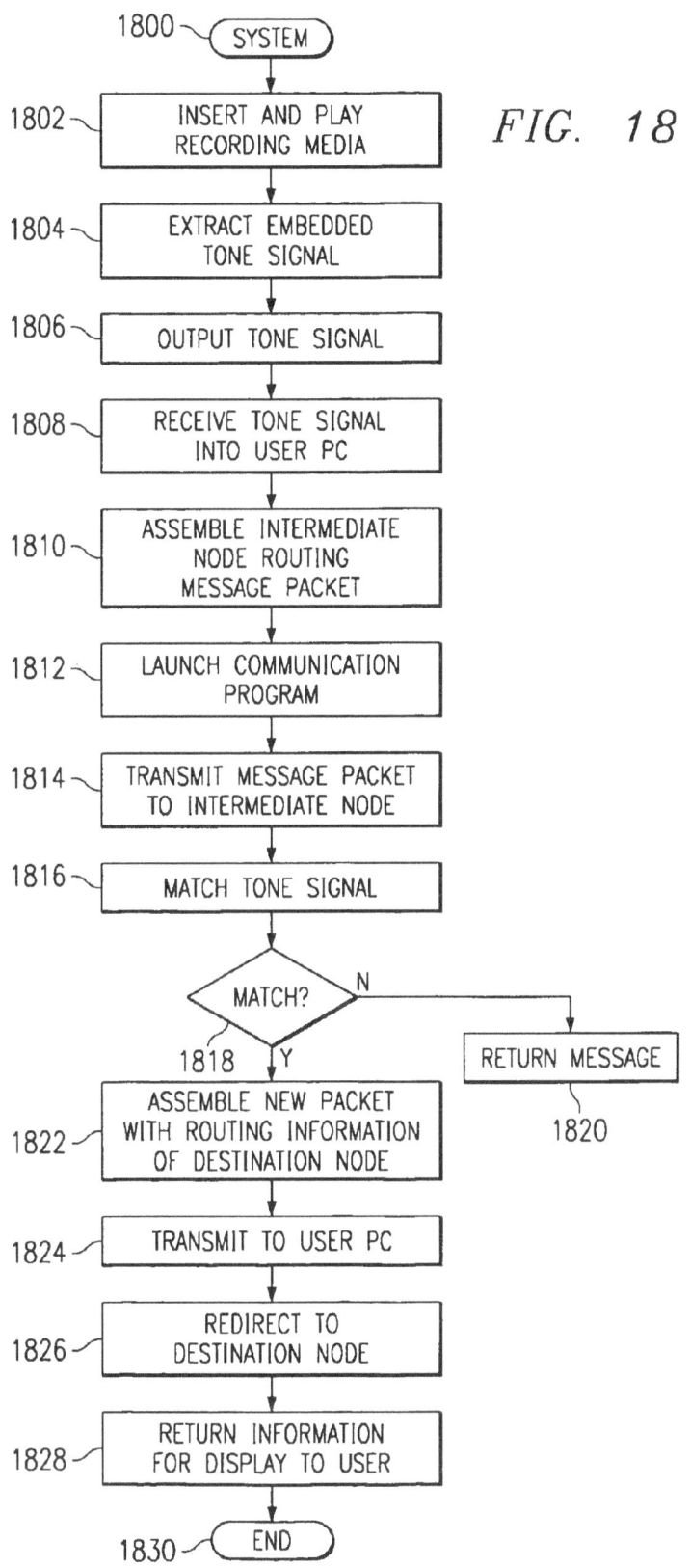

*FIG. 18*

1800 — SYSTEM

1802 — INSERT AND PLAY RECORDING MEDIA

1804 — EXTRACT EMBEDDED TONE SIGNAL

1806 — OUTPUT TONE SIGNAL

1808 — RECEIVE TONE SIGNAL INTO USER PC

1810 — ASSEMBLE INTERMEDIATE NODE ROUTING MESSAGE PACKET

1812 — LAUNCH COMMUNICATION PROGRAM

1814 — TRANSMIT MESSAGE PACKET TO INTERMEDIATE NODE

1816 — MATCH TONE SIGNAL

1818 — MATCH?

N — RETURN MESSAGE
1820

Y

1822 — ASSEMBLE NEW PACKET WITH ROUTING INFORMATION OF DESTINATION NODE

1824 — TRANSMIT TO USER PC

1826 — REDIRECT TO DESTINATION NODE

1828 — RETURN INFORMATION FOR DISPLAY TO USER

1830 — END

1

# METHOD OF CONTROLLING A COMPUTER USING AN EMBEDDED UNIQUE CODE IN THE CONTENT OF DVD MEDIA

## CROSS REFERENCE TO RELATED APPLICATION

This application is a Continuation-in-Part of U.S. patent application Ser. No. 09/151,530, entitled "METHOD AND APPARATUS FOR CONTROLLING A COMPUTER WITH AN AUDIO SIGNAL" filed Sep. 11, 1998, and now issued on Aug. 1, 2000 as U.S. Pat. No. 6,098,106; and is related to the following U.S. patent applications: Ser. No. 09/151,471 entitled "METHOD FOR INTERFACING SCANNED PRODUCT INFORMATION WITH A SOURCE FOR THE PRODUCT OVER A GLOBAL NET-WORK" filed Sep. 11, 1998; Ser. No. 09/378,222 entitled, "METHOD AND APPARATUS FOR EMBEDDING ROUTING INFORMATION TO A REMOTE WEB SITE IN AN AUDIO/VIDEO TRACK" filed on Aug. 19, 1999; Ser. No. 09/378,220 entitled "METHOD AND APPARA-TUS FOR CONTROLLING A USER'S COMPUTER FROM A REMOTE LOCATION" filed on Aug. 19, 1999; Ser. No. 09/378,216 entitled "METHOD FOR CONTROL-LING A COMPUTER USING AN EMBEDDED UNIQUE CODE IN THE CONTENT OF VIDEO TAPE MEDIA" filed on Aug. 19, 1999; Ser. No. 09/378,217 entitled "METHOD FOR CONTROLLING A COMPUTER USING AN EMBEDDED UNIQUE CODE IN THE CONTENT OF CD MEDIA" filed on Aug. 19, 1999; Ser. No. 09/378,215 entitled "METHOD FOR CONTROLLING A COMPUTER USING AN EMBEDDED UNIQUE CODE IN THE CON-TENT OF DAT MEDIA" filed on Aug. 19, 1999.

## TECHNICAL FIELD OF THE INVENTION

This invention is related to a method of computer control, and particularly for automatically directing a web browser application on the computer to retrieve and display infor-mation in response to an analog signal.

## BACKGROUND OF THE INVENTION

With the growing numbers of computer users connecting to the "Internet," many companies are seeking the substan-tial commercial opportunities presented by such a large user base. For example, one technology which exists allows a television ("TV") signal to trigger a computer response in which the consumer will be guided to a personalized web page. The source of the triggering signal may be a TV, video tape recorder, or radio. For example, if a viewer is watching a TV program in which an advertiser offers viewer voting, the advertiser may transmit a unique signal within the television signal which controls a program known as a "browser" on the viewer's computer to automatically dis-play the advertiser's web page. The viewer then simply makes a selection which is then transmitted back to the advertiser.

In order to provide the viewer with the capability of responding to a wide variety of companies using this tech-nology, a database of company information and Uniform Resource Locator ("URL") codes is necessarily maintained in the viewer's computer, requiring continuous updates. URLs are short strings of data that identify resources on the Internet: documents, images, downloadable files, services, electronic mailboxes, and other resources. URLs make resources available under a variety of naming schemes and

2

access methods such as HTTP, FTP, and Internet mail, addressable in the same simple way. URLs reduce the tedium of "login to this server, then issue this magic com-mand . . . " down to a single click. The Internet uses URLs to specify the location of files on other servers. A URL includes the type of resource being accessed (e.g., Web, gopher, FTP), the address of the server, and the location of the file. The URL can point to any file on any networked computer. Current technology requires the viewer to per-form periodic updates to obtain the most current URL database. This aspect of the current technology is cumber-some since the update process requires downloading infor-mation to the viewer's computer. Moreover, the likelihood for error in performing the update, and the necessity of redoing the update in the event of a later computer crash, further complicates the process. Additionally, current tech-nologies are limited in the number of companies which may be stored in the database. This is a significant limitation since world-wide access presented by the Internet and the increasing number of companies connecting to perform on-line commerce necessitates a large database.

## SUMMARY OF THE INVENTION

The present invention disclosed and claimed herein com-prises a method for controlling a computer via a unique code which is embedded in the content of recorded information of a digital video disk. The unique code in close association with vendor information. The unique code is extracted with an extractor during output of the recorded information to a user at a user location disposed on a network. In response to extracting the unique code, the unique code is transmitted to a remote location on the network in accordance with routing information stored at the user location, wherein the vendor information is returned to the user location for processing.

## BRIEF DESCRIPTION OF THE DRAWINGS

For a more complete understanding of the present inven-tion and the advantages thereof, reference is now made to the following description taken in conjunction with the accompanying Drawings in which:

FIG. 1 illustrates a block diagram of the preferred embodiment;

FIG. 2 illustrates the computer components employed in this embodiment;

FIG. 3 illustrates system interactions over a global net-work;

FIGS. 4a–4e illustrate the various message packets trans-mitted between the source PC and network servers used in the preferred embodiment;

FIG. 5 is a flowchart depicting operation of the system according to the preferred embodiment;

FIG. 6 illustrates a flowchart of actions taken by the Advertiser Reference Server ("ARS") server;

FIG. 7 illustrates a flowchart of the interactive process between the source computer and ARS;

FIG. 8 illustrates a web browser page receiving the modified URL/advertiser product data according to the preferred embodiment;

FIG. 9 illustrates a simplified block diagram of the disclosed embodiment;

FIG. 10 illustrates a more detailed, simplified block diagram of the embodiment of FIG. 9;

FIG. 11 illustrates a diagrammatic view of a method for performing the routing operation;

FIG. 12 illustrates a block diagram of an alternate embodiment utilizing an optical region in the video image for generating the routing information;

FIG. 13 illustrates a block diagram illustrating the generation of a profile with the disclosed embodiment;

FIG. 14 illustrates a flowchart for generating the profile and storing at the ARS;

FIG. 15 illustrates a flowchart for processing the profile information when information is routed to a user;

FIG. 16 illustrates a block diagram according to an alternative embodiment;

FIG. 17 illustrates a diagrammatic view of the interconnection with the network in the disclosure of FIG. 16; and

FIG. 18 illustrates a flowchart depicting the operation at the recording media architecture.

## DETAILED DESCRIPTION OF THE INVENTION

Referring now to FIG. 1, there is illustrated a block diagram of a system for controlling a personal computer ("PC") 112 via an audio tone transmitted over a wireless system utilizing a TV. In the embodiment illustrated in FIG. 1, there is provided a transmission station 101 and a receive station 117 that are connected via a communication link 108. The transmission station 101 is comprised of a television program source 104, which is operable to generate a program in the form of a broadcast signal comprised of video and audio. This is transmitted via conventional techniques along channels in the appropriate frequencies. The program source is input to a mixing device 106, which mixing device is operable to mix in an audio signal. This audio signal is derived from an audio source 100 which comprises a coded audio signal which is then modulated onto a carrier which is combined with the television program source 104. This signal combining can be done at the audio level, or it can even be done at the RF level in the form of a different carrier. However, the preferred method is to merely sum the audio signal from the modulator 102 into the audio channel of the program that is generated by the television program source 104. The output thereof is provided from the mixing device 106 in the form of broadcast signal to an antenna 107, which transmits the information over the communication link 108 to an antenna 109 on the receive side.

On the receive side of the system, a conventional receiver 110, such as a television is provided. This television provides a speaker output which provides the user with an audible signal. This is typically associated with the program. However, the receiver 110 in the disclosed embodiment, also provides an audio output jack, this being the type RCA jack. This jack is utilized to provide an audio output signal on a line 113 which is represented by an audio signal 111. This line 113 provides all of the audio that is received over the communication link 108 to the PC 112 in the audio input port on the PC 112. However, it should be understood that, although a direct connection is illustrated from the receiver 110 to the PC 112, there actually could be a microphone pickup at the PC 112 which could pick the audio signal up. In the disclosed embodiment the audio signal generated by the advertiser data input device 100 is audible to the human ear and, therefore, can be heard by the user. Therefore, no special filters are needed to provide this audio to the PC 112.

The PC 112 is operable to run programs thereon which typically are stored in a program file area 116. These programs can be any type of programs such as word processing programs, application programs, etc. In the disclosed embodiment, the program that is utilized in the

system is what is referred to as a "browser." The PC 112 runs a browser program to facilitate the access of information on the network, for example, a global communication network known as the "Internet" or the World-Wide-Web ("Web"). The browser is a hypertext-linked application used for accessing information. Hypertext is a term used to describe a particular organization of information within a data processing system, and its presentation to a user. It exploits the computer's ability to link together information from a wide variety of sources to provide the user with the ability to explore a particular topic. The traditional style of presentation used in books employs an organization of the information which is imposed upon it by limitations of the medium, namely fixed sized, sequential paper pages. Hypertext systems, however, use a large number of units of text or other types of data such as image information, graphical information, video information, or sound information, which can vary in size. A collection of such units of information is termed a hypertext document, or where the hypertext documents employ information other than text, hypermedia documents. Multimedia communications may use the Hypertext Transfer Protocol ("HTTP"), and files or formatted data may use the Hypertext Markup Language ("HTML"). This formatting language provides for a mingling of text, graphics, sound, video, and hypertext links by "tagging" a text document using HTML. Data encoded using HTML is often referred to as an "HTML document," an "HTML page," or a "home page." These documents and other Internet resources may be accessed across the network by means of a network addressing scheme which uses a locator referred to as a Uniform Resource Locator ("URL"), for example, "http://www.digital.com."

The Internet is one of the most utilized networks for interconnecting distributed computer systems and allows users of these computer systems to exchange data all over the world. Connected to the Internet are many private networks, for example, corporate or commercial networks. Standard protocols, such as the Transport Control Protocol ("TCP") and the Internet Protocol ("IP") provide a convenient method for communicating across these diverse networks. These protocols dictate how data are formatted and communicated. As a characteristic of the Internet, the protocols are layered in an IP stack. At higher levels of the IP stack, such as the application layer (where HTTP is employed), the user information is more readily visible, while at lower levels, such as the network level (where TCP/IP are used), the data can merely be observed as packets or a stream of rapidly moving digital signals. Superimposed on the Internet is a standard protocol interface for accessing Web resources, such as servers, files, Web pages, mail messages, and the like. One way that Web resources can be accessed is by browsers made by Netscape® and Microsoft Internet Explorer®.

Referring again now to FIG. 1, the user can load this program with the appropriate keystrokes such that a browser window will be displayed on a display 118. In one embodiment, the user can run the browser program on the PC 112 such that the browser window is displayed on the display 118. While watching a preferred program, the user can also view display 118. When an audio signal is received by the receiver 110 and the encoded information is contained therein that was input thereto by the advertiser, the PC 112 will then perform a number of operations. The first operation, according to the disclosed embodiment, is to extract the audio information within the received audio signal in the form of digital data, and then transmit this digital data to a defined location on the global communication network via a

modem connection **114**. This connection will be described hereinbelow. This information will be relayed to a proprietary location and the instructions sent back to the PC **112** as to the location of the advertiser associated with the code, and the PC **112** will then effect a communication link to that location such that the user can view on the display **118** information that the advertiser, by the fact of putting the tone onto the broadcast channel, desires the viewer to view. This information can be in the form of interactive programs, data files, etc. In one example, when an advertisement appears on the television, the tone can be generated and then additional data displayed on the display **118**. Additionally, a streaming video program could be played on the PC received over the network, which streaming video program is actually longer than the advertising segment on the broadcast. Another example would be a sports game that would broadcast the tone in order to allow a user access to information that is not available over the broadcast network, such as additional statistics associated with the sports program, etc.

By utilizing the system described herein with respect to the disclosed embodiment of FIG. 1, an advertiser is allowed the ability to control a user's PC **112** through the use of tones embedded within a program audio signal. As will described hereinbelow, the disclosed embodiment utilizes particular routing information stored in the PC **112** which allows the encoded information in the received audio signal to route this information to a desired location on the network, and then allow other routing information to be returned to the PC **112** for control thereof to route the PC **112** to the appropriate location associated with that code.

Referring now to FIG. **2**, there is illustrated a computer **204**, similar to computer **112**, connected to display information on display **118**. The computer **204** comprises an internal audio or "sound" card **206** for receiving the transmitted audio signal through receive antenna **109** and receiver **110**. The sound card **206** typically contains analog-to-digital circuitry for converting the analog audio signal into a digital signal. The digital signal may then be more easily manipulated by software programs. The receiver **110** separates the audio signal from the video signal. A special trigger signal located within the transmitted advertiser audio signal triggers proprietary software running on the computer **204** which launches a communication application, in this particular embodiment, the web browser application located on the PC **204**. Coded advertiser information contained within the audio signal is then extracted and appended with the address of a proprietary server located on the communication network. The remote server address is in the form of a URL. This appended data, in addition to other control codes, is inserted directly into the web browser application for automatic routing to the communication network. The web browser running on PC **204**, and communicating to the network with an internal modem **208**, in this embodiment, transmits the advertiser information to the remote server. The remote server cross-references the advertiser product information to the address of the advertiser server located on the network. The address of the advertiser server is routed back through the PC **204** web browser to the advertiser server. The advertiser product information is returned to PC **204** to be presented to the viewer on display **118**. In this particular embodiment, the particular advertiser product information displayed is contained within the advertiser's web page **212**. As mentioned above, the audio signal is audible to the human ear. Therefore the audio signal, as emitted from the TV speakers, may be input to the sound card **206** via a microphone. Furthermore, the audio signal need not be a real-time broadcast, but may be on video tapes,

CDs, DVD, or other media which may be displayed at a later date. With the imminent implementation of high definition digital television, the audio signal output from the TV may also be digital. Therefore, direct input into a sound card for A/D purposes may not be necessary, but alternative interfacing techniques to accommodate digital-to-digital signal formats would apply.

Referring now to FIG. **3**, there is illustrated a source PC **302**, similar to PCs **204** and **112**, connected to a global communication network (GCN) **306** through an interface **304**. In this embodiment, the audio signal **111** is received by PC **302** through its sound card **206**. The audio signal **111** comprises a trigger signal which triggers proprietary software into launching a web browser application residing on the PC **302**. The audio signal **111** also comprises advertiser product information which is extracted and appended with URL information of an Advertiser Reference Server ("ARS") **308**. The ARS **308** is a system disposed on the network **306** that is defined as the location to which data in the audio signal **111** is to be routed. As such, data in the audio signal **111** will always be routed to the ARS **308**, since a URL is unique on the GCN **306**. Connected to the ARS **308** is a database **310** of product codes and associated manufacturer URLs. The database **310** undergoes a continual update process which is transparent to the user. As companies sign-on, i.e., subscribe, to this technology, manufacturer and product information is added to the database **310** without interrupting operation of the source PC **302** with frequent updates. When the advertiser server address URL is obtained from the ARS database **310**, it and the request for the particular advertiser product information are automatically routed back through the web browser on PC **302**, over to the respective advertiser server for retrieval of the advertiser product information to the PC **302**. Additionally, that although the disclosed invention discusses a global communication network, the system is also applicable to LANs, WANs, and peer-to-peer network configurations. It should be noted that the disclosed architecture is not limited to a single source PC **302**, but may comprise a plurality of source PCs, e.g., PC **300** and PC **303**. Moreover, a plurality of ARS **308** systems and advertiser servers **312** may be implemented, e.g., ARS **314**, and advertiser server A **316**, respectively.

The information transactions, in general, which occur between the networked systems of this embodiment, over the communication network, are the following. The web browser running on source PC **302** transmits a message packet to the ARS **308** over Path "A." The ARS **308** decodes the message packet and performs a cross-reference function with product information extracted from the received message packet to obtain the address of an advertiser server **312**. A new message packet is assembled comprising the advertiser server **312** address, and sent back to the source PC **302** over Path "B." A "handoff" operation is performed whereby the source PC **302** browser simply reroutes the information on to the advertiser server **312** over Path "C," with the appropriate source and destination address appended. The advertiser server **312** receives and decodes the message packet. The request-for-advertiser-product-information is extracted and the advertiser **312** retrieves the requested information from its database for transmission back to the source PC **302** over Path "D." The source PC **302** then processes the information, i.e., for display to the viewer. The optional Path "E" is discussed hereinbelow. It should be noted that the disclosed methods are not limited to only browser communication applications, but may accommodate, with sufficient modifications by one skilled in the art,

other communication applications used to transmit information over the Internet or communication network.

Referring now to FIG. 4*a*, the message packet 400 sent from the source PC 302 to ARS 308 via Path "A" comprises several fields. One field comprises the URL of the ARS 308 which indicates where the message packet is to be sent. Another field comprises the advertiser product code or other information derived from the audio signal 111, and any additional overhead information required for a given transaction. The product code provides a link to the address of the advertiser server 312, located in the database 310. Yet another field comprises the network address of the source PC 302. In general, network transmissions are effected in packets of information, each packet providing a destination address, a source address, and data. These packets vary depending upon the network transmission protocol utilized for communication. Although the protocols utilized in the disclosed embodiment are of a conventional protocol suite commonly known as TCP/IP, it should be understood that any protocols providing the similar basic functions can be used, with the primary requirement that a browser can forward the routing information to the desired URL in response to keystrokes being input to a PC. However, it should be understood that any protocol can be used, with the primary requirement that a browser can forward the product information to the desired URL in response to keystrokes being input to a PC. Within the context of this disclosure, "message packet" shall refer to and comprise the destination URL, product information, and source address, even though more than a single packet must be transmitted to effect such a transmission.

Upon receipt of the message packet 400 from source PC 302, ARS 308 processes the information in accordance with instructions embedded in the overhead information. The ARS 308 specifically will extract the product code information from the received packet 400 and, once extracted, will then decode this product code information. Once decoded, this information is then compared with data contained within the ARS advertiser database 310 to determine if there is a "hit." If there is no "hit" indicating a match, then information is returned to the browser indicating such. If there is a "hit," a packet 402 is assembled which comprises the address of the source PC 302, and information instructing the source PC 302 as to how to access, directly in a "handoff" operation, another location on the network, that of an advertiser server 312. This type of construction is relatively conventional with browsers such as Netscape® and Microsoft Internet Explorer® and, rather than displaying information from the ARS 308, the source PC 302 can then access the advertiser server 312. The ARS 308 transmits the packet 402 back to source PC 302 over Path "B." Referring now to FIG. 4*b*, the message packet 402 comprises the address of the source PC 302, the URL of the advertiser server 312 embedded within instructional code, and the URL of the ARS 308.

Upon receipt of the message packet 402 by the source PC 302, the message packet 402 is disassembled to obtain pertinent routing information for assembly of a new message packet 404. The web browser running on source PC 302 is now directed to obtain, over Path "C," the product information relevant to the particular advertiser server 312 location information embedded in message packet 404. Referring now to FIG. 4*c*, the message packet 404 for this transaction comprises the URL of the advertiser server 312, the request-for-product-information data, and the address of the source PC 302.

## 8

Upon receipt of the message packet 404 from source PC 302, advertiser server 312 disassembles the message packet 404 to obtain the request-for-product-information data. The advertiser server 312 then retrieves the particular product information from its database, and transmits it over Path "D" back to the source PC 302. Referring now to FIG. 4*d*, the message packet 406 for this particular transaction comprises the address of the source PC 302, the requested information, and the URL of the advertiser server 312.

Optionally, the ARS 308 may make a direct request for product information over Path "E" to advertiser server 312. In this mode, the ARS 308 sends information to the advertiser server 312 instructing it to contact the source PC 302. This, however, is unconventional and requires more complex software control. The message packet 408 for this transaction is illustrated in FIG. 4*e*, which comprises the URL of the advertiser server 312, the request-for-product-information data, and the address of the source PC 302. Since product information is not being returned to the ARS 308, but directly to the source PC 302, the message packet 408 requires the return address to be that of the source PC 302. The product information is then passed directly to PC 302 over Path "D."

Referring now to FIG. 5, the method for detecting and obtaining product information is as follows. In decision block 500, a proprietary application running resident on a source computer PC 302 (similar to PC 204) monitors the audio input for a special trigger signal. Upon detection of the trigger signal, data following the trigger signal is decoded for further processing, in function block 502. In function block 504, the data is buffered for further manipulation. In decision block 506, a determination is made as to whether the data can be properly authenticated. If not, program flow continues through the "N" signal to function block 520 where the data is discarded. In function block 522, the program then signals for a retransmission of the data. The system then waits for the next trigger signal, in decision block 500. If properly authenticated in decision block 506, program flow continues through the "Y" signal path where the data is then used to launch the web browser application, as indicated in function block 508. In function block 510, the web browser receives the URL data, which is then automatically routed through the computer modem 208 to the network interface 304 and ultimately to the network 306. In function block 514, the ARS 308 responds by returning the URL of advertiser server 312 to the PC 302. In function block 516, the web browser running on the source PC 302, receives the advertiser URL information from the ARS 308, and transmits the URL for the product file to the advertiser server 312. In block 518, the advertiser server 312 responds by sending the product information to the source PC 302 for processing.

The user may obtain the benefits of this architecture by simply downloading the proprietary software over the network. Other methods for obtaining the software are well-known; for example, by CD, diskette, or pre-loaded hard drives.

Referring now to FIG. 6, there is illustrated a flowchart of the process the ARS 308 may undergo when receiving the message packet 400 from the source PC 302. In decision block 600, the ARS 308 checks for the receipt of the message packet 400. If a message packet 400 is not received, program flow moves along the "N" path to continue waiting for the message. If the message packet 400 is received, program flow continues along path "Y" for message processing. Upon receipt of the message packet 400, in function block 602, the ARS 308 decodes the message packet 400.

## 9

The product code is then extracted independently in function block **604** in preparation for matching the product code with the appropriate advertiser server address located in the database **310**. In function block **606**, the product code is then used with a look-up table to retrieve the advertiser server **312** URL of the respective product information contained in the audio signal data. In function block **608**, the ARS **308** then assembles message packet **402** for transmission back to the source PC **302**. Function block **610** indicates the process of sending the message packet **402** back to the source PC **302** over Path "B."

Referring now to FIG. **7**, there is illustrated a flowchart of the interactive processes between the source PC **302** and the advertiser server **312**. In function block **700**, the source PC **302** receives the message packet **402** back from the ARS **308** and begins to decode the packet **402**. In function block **702**, the URL of the advertiser product information is extracted from the message packet **402** and saved for insertion into the message packet **404** to the advertiser server **312**. The message packet **404** is then assembled and sent by the source PC **302** over Path "C" to the advertiser server **312**, in function block **704**. While the source PC **302** waits, in function block **706**, the advertiser server **312** receives the message packet **404** from the source PC **302**, in function block **708**, and disassembles it. The product information location is then extracted from the message packet **404** in function block **710**. The particular product information is retrieved from the advertiser server **312** database for transmission back to the source PC **302**. In function block **712**, the product information is assembled into message packet **406** and then transmitted back to the source PC **302** over Path "D." Returning to the source PC **302** in function block **714**, the advertiser product information contained in the message packet **406** received from the advertiser server **312**, is then extracted and processed in function block **716**.

Referring now to FIG. **8**, after receipt of a trigger signal, a web browser application on a source PC **302** is automatically launched and computer display **800** presents a browser page **802**. Proprietary software running on the source PC **302** processes the audio signal data after being digitized through the sound card **206**. The software appropriately prepares the data for insertion directly into the web browser by extracting the product information code and appending keystroke data to this information. First, a URL page **804** is opened in response to a Ctrl-O command added by the proprietary software as the first character string. Opening URL page **804** automatically positions the cursor in a field **806** where additional keystroke data following the Ctrl-O command will be inserted. After URL page **804** is opened, the hypertext protocol preamble http:// is inserted into the field **806**. Next, URL information associated with the location of the ARS **308** is inserted into field **806**. Following the ARS **308** URL data are the characters /? to allow entry of variables immediately following the /? characters. In this embodiment, the variable following is the product information code received in the audio signal. The product code information also provides the cross-reference information for obtaining the advertiser URL from the ARS database **310**. Next, a carriage return is added to send the URL/ product data and close the window **804**. After the message packet **400** is transmitted to the ARS **308** from the source PC **302**, transactions from the ARS **308**, to the source PC **302**, to the advertiser server **312**, and back to the source PC **302**, occur quickly and are transparent to the viewer. At this point, the next information the viewer sees is the product information which was received from the advertiser server **312**.

## 10

Referring now to FIG. **9**, there is illustrated a block diagram of a more simplified embodiment. In this embodiment, a video source **902** is provided which is operable to provide an audio output on an audio cable **901** which provides routing information referred to by reference numeral **904**. The routing information **904** is basically information contained within the audio signal. This is an encoded or embedded signal. The important aspect of the routing information **904** is that it is automatically output in realtime as a function of the broadcast of the video program received over the video source **902**. Therefore, whenever the program is being broadcast in realtime to the user **908**, the routing information **904** will be output whenever the producer of the video desires it to be produced. It should be understood that the box **902** representing the video source could be any type of media that will result in the routing information being output. This could be a cassette player, a DVD player, an audio cassette, a CD ROM or any such media. It is only important that this is a program that the producer develops which the user **908** watches in a continuous or a streaming manner. Embedded within that program, at a desired point selected by the producer, the routing information **904** is output.

The audio information is then routed to a PC **906**, which is similar to the PC **112** in FIG. **1**. A user **908** is interfaced with the PC to receive information thereof, the PC **906** having associated therewith a display (not shown). The PC **906** is interfaced with a network **910**, similar to the network **306** in FIG. **3**. This network **910** has multiple nodes thereon, one of which is the PC **906**, and another of which is represented by a network node **912** which represents remote information. The object of the present embodiment is to access remote information for display to the user **908** by the act of transmitting from the video program in block **902** the routing information **904**. This routing information **904** is utilized to allow the PC **906** which has a network "browser" running thereon to "fetch" the remote information at the node **912** over the network **910** for display to the user **908**. This routing information **904** is in the form of an embedded code within the audio signal, as was described hereinabove.

Referring now to FIG. **10**, there is illustrated a more detailed block diagram of the embodiment of FIG. **9**. In this embodiment, the PC **906** is split up into a couple of nodes, a first PC **1002** and a second PC **1004**. The PC **1002** resides at the node associated with the user **908**, and the PC **1004** resides at another node. The PC **1004** represents the ARS **308** of FIG. **3**. The PC **1004** has a database **1006** associated therewith, which is basically the advertiser database **310**. Therefore, there are three nodes on the network **910** necessary to implement the disclosed embodiment, the PC **1002**, the PC **1004** and the remote information node **912**. The routing information **904** is utilized by the PC **1002** for routing to the PC **1004** to determine the location of the remote information node **912** on the network **910**. This is returned to the PC **1002** and a connection made directly with the remote information node **912** and the information retrieved therefrom to the user **908**. The routing information **904** basically constitutes primary routing information.

Referring now to FIG. **11**, there is illustrated a diagrammatic view of how the network packet is formed for sending the primary routing information to the PC **1004**. In general, the primary routing information occupies a single field which primary routing information is then assembled into a data packet with the secondary routing information for transfer to the network **910**. This is described hereinabove in detail.

## 11

Referring now to FIG. **12**, there is illustrated an alternate embodiment to that of FIG. **9**. In this embodiment, the video source **902** has associated therewith an optical region **1202**, which optical region **1202** has disposed therein an embedded video code. This embedded video code could be relatively complex or as simple as a grid of dark and white regions, each region in the grid able to have a dark color for a logic "1" or a white region for a logic "0." This will allow a digital value to be disposed within the optical region **1202**. A sensor **1204** can then be provided for sensing this video code. In the example above, this would merely require an array of optical detectors, one for each region in the grid to determine whether this is a logic "1" or a logic "0" state. One of the sensed video is then output to the PC **906** for processing thereof to determine the information contained therein, which information contained therein constitutes the primary routing information **904**. Thereafter, it is processed as described hereinabove with reference to FIG. **9**.

Referring now to FIG. **13**, there is illustrated a block diagram for an embodiment wherein a user's profile can be forwarded to the original subscriber or manufacturer. The PC **906** has associated therewith a profile database **1302**, which profile database **1302** is operable to store a profile of the user **908**. This profile is created when the program, after initial installation, requests profile information to be input in order to activate the program. In addition to the profile, there is also a unique ID that is provided to the user **908** in association with the browser program that runs on the PC **906**. This is stored in a storage location represented by a block **1304**. This ID **1304** is accessible by a remote location as a "cookie" which is information that is stored in the PC **906** in an accessible location, which accessible location is actually accessible by the remote program running on a remote node.

The ARS **308**, which basically constitutes the PC **1004** of FIG. **10**, is operable to have associated therewith a profile database **1308**, which profile database **1308** is operable to store profiles for all of the users. The profile database **1308** is a combination of the information stored in profile database **1302** for all of the PCs **906** that are attachable to the system. This is to be distinguished from information stored in the database **310** of the ARS **308**, the advertiser's database, which contains intermediate destination tables. When the routing information in the primary routing information **904** is forwarded to the ARS **308** and extracted from the original data packet, the look-up procedure described hereinabove can then be performed to determine where this information is to be routed. The profile database **1302** is then utilized for each transaction, wherein each transaction in the form of the routing information received from the primary routing information **904** is compared to the destination tables of database **310** to determine what manufacturer is associated therewith. The associated ID **1304** that is transmitted along with the routing information in primary routing information **904** is then compared with the profile database **1308** to determine if a profile associated therewith is available. This information is stored in a transaction database **1310** such that, at a later time, for each routing code received in the form of the information in primary routing information **904**, there will associated therewith the IDs **1304** of each of the PCs **906**. The associated profiles in database **1308**, which are stored in association with IDs **1304**, can then be assembled and transmitted to a subscriber as referenced by a subscriber node **1312** on the network **910**. The ARS **308** can do this in two modes, a realtime mode or a non-realtime mode. In a realtime mode, each time a PC **906** accesses the advertiser database **310**, that user's profile information is uploaded to

the subscriber node **1312**. At the same time, billing information is generated for that subscriber **1312** which is stored in a billing database **1316**. Therefore, the ARS **308** has the ability to inform the subscriber **1312** of each transaction, bill for those transactions, and also provide to the subscriber **1312** profile information regarding who is accessing the particular product advertisement having associated therewith the routing information field **904** for a particular routing code as described hereinabove. This information, once assembled, can then be transmitted to the subscriber **1312** and also be reflected in billing information and stored in the billing information database **1316**.

Referring now to FIG. **14**, there is illustrated a flowchart depicting the operation for storing the profile for the user. The program is initiated in a block **1402** and then proceeds to a function block **1404**, wherein the system will prompt for the profile upon initiation of the system. This initiation is a function that is set to activate whenever the user initially loads the software that he or she is provided. The purpose for this is to create, in addition to the setup information, a user profile. Once the user is prompted for this, then the program will flow to a decision block **1406** to determine whether the user provides basic or detailed information. This is selectable by the user. If selecting basic, the program will flow to a function block **1408** wherein the user will enter basic information such as name and serial number and possibly an address. However, to provide some incentive to the user to enter more information, the original prompt in function block **1404** would have offers for such things as coupons, discounts, etc., if the user will enter additional information. If the user selects this option, the program flows from the decision block **1406** to a function block **1410**. In the function block **1410**, the user is prompted to enter specific information such as job, income level, general family history, demographic information and more. There can be any amount of information collected in this particular function block.

Once all of the information is collected, in either the basic mode or the more specific mode, the program will then flow to a function block **1412** where this information is stored locally. The program then flows to a decision block **1414** to then go on-line to the host or the ARS **308**. In general, the user is prompted to determine whether he or she wants to send this information to the host at the present time or to send it later. If he or she selects the "later" option, the program will flow to a function block **1415** to prompt the user at a later time to send the information. In the disclosed embodiment, the user will not be able to utilize the software until the profile information is sent to the host. Therefore, the user may have to activate this at a later time in order to connect with the host.

If the user has selected the option to upload the profile information to the host, the program will flow to the function block **1416** to initiate the connect process and then to a decision block **1418** to determine if the connection has been made. If not, the program will flow along a "N" path to a decision block **1420** which will timeout to an error block **1422** or back to the input of the connect decision block **1418**. The program, once connected, will then flow along a "Y" path from decision block **1418** to a function block **1428** to send the profile information with the ID of the computer or user to the host. The ID is basically, as described hereinabove, a "cookie" in the computer which is accessed by the program when transmitting to the host. The program will then flow to a function block **1430** to activate the program such that it, at later time, can operate without requiring all of the setup information. In general, all of the operation of

this flowchart is performed with a "wizard" which steps the user through the setup process. Once complete, the program will flow to a Done block **1432**.

Referring now to FIG. **15**, there is illustrated a flowchart depicting the operation of the host when receiving a transaction. The program is initiated at a Start block **1502** and then proceeds to decision block **1504**, wherein it is determined whether the system has received a routing request, i.e., the routing information **904** in the form of a tone, etc., embedded in the audio signal, as described hereinabove with respect to FIG. **9**. The program will loop back around to the input of decision block **1504** until the routing request has been received. At this time, the program will flow along the "Y" path to a function block **1506** to receive the primary routing information and the user ID. Essentially, this primary routing information is extracted from the audio tone, in addition to the user ID. The program then flows to a function block **1508** to look up the manufacturer URL that corresponds to the received primary routing information and then return the necessary command information to the originating PC **112** in order to allow that PC **112** to connect to the destination associated with the primary routing information. Thereafter, the program will flow to a function block **1510** to update the transaction database **1310** for the current transaction. In general, the routing information **904** will be stored as a single field with the associated IDs. The profile database **1308**, as described hereinabove, has associated therewith detailed profiles of each user on the system that has activated their software in association with their ID. Since the ID was sent in association with the routing information, what is stored in the transaction database **1310** is the routing code, in association with all of the IDs transmitted to the system in association with that particular routing code. Once this transaction database **1310** has been updated, as described hereinabove, the transactions can be transferred back to the subscriber at node **312** with the detailed profile information from the profile database **1308**.

The profile information can be transmitted back to the subscriber or manufacturer at the node **312** in realtime or non-realtime. A decision block **1512** is provided for this, which determines if the delivery is realtime. If realtime, the program will flow along a "Y" path to a function block **1514** wherein the information will be immediately forwarded to the manufacturer or subscriber. The program will then flow to a function block **1516** wherein the billing for that particular manufacturer or subscriber will be updated in the billing database **1316**. The program will then flow into an End block **1518**. If it was non-realtime, the program moves along the "N" path to a function block **1520** wherein it is set for a later delivery and it is accrued in the transaction database **1310**. In any event, the transaction database **1310** will accrue all information associated with a particular routing code.

With a realtime transaction, it is possible for a manufacturer to place an advertisement in a magazine or to place a product on a shelf at a particular time. The manufacturer can thereafter monitor the times when either the advertisements are or the products are purchased. Of course, they must be scanned into a computer which will provide some delay. However, the manufacturer can gain a very current view of how a product is moving. For example, if a cola manufacturer were to provide a promotional advertisement on, for example, television, indicating that a new cola was going to be placed on the shelf and that the first 1000 purchasers, for example, scanning their code into the network would receive some benefit, such as a chance to win a trip to some famous resort in Florida or some other incentive, the manufacturer

would have a very good idea as to how well the advertisement was received. Further, the advertiser would know where the receptive markets were. If this advertiser, for example, had placed the television advertisement in ten cities and received overwhelming response from one city, but very poor response from another city, he would then have some inclination to believe that either the one poor-response city was not a good market or that the advertising medium he had chosen was very poor. Since the advertiser can obtain a relatively instant response and also content with that response as to the demographics of the responder, very important information can be obtained in a relatively short time.

It should be noted that the disclosed embodiment is not limited to a single source PC **302**, but may encompass a large number of source computers connected over a global communication network. Additionally, the embodiment is not limited to a single ARS **308** or a single advertiser server **312**, but may include a plurality of ARS and advertiser systems, indicated by the addition of ARS **314** and advertiser server A **316**, respectively. It should also be noted that this embodiment is not limited only to global communication networks, but also may be used with LAN, WAN, and peer-to-peer configurations.

It should also be noted that the disclosed embodiment is not limited to a personal computer, but is also applicable to, for example, a Network Computer ("NetPC"), a scaled-down version of the PC, or any system which accommodates user interaction and interfaces to information resources.

One typical application of the above noted technique is for providing a triggering event during a program, such as a sport event. In a first example, this may be generated by an advertiser. One could imagine that, due to the cost of advertisements in a high profile sports program, there is a desire to utilize this time wisely. If, for example, an advertiser contracted for 15 seconds worth of advertising time, they could insert within their program a tone containing the routing information. This routing information can then be output to the user's PC **302** which will cause the user's PC **302** to, via the network, obtain information from a remote location typically controlled by the advertiser. This could be in the form of an advertisement of a length longer than that contracted for. Further, this could be an interactive type of advertisement. An important aspect to the type of interaction between the actual broadcast program with the embedded routing information and the manufacturer's site is the fact that there is provided information as to the user's PC **302** and a profile of the user themselves. Therefore, an advertiser can actually gain realtime information as to the number of individuals that are watching their particular advertisement and also information as to the background of those individuals, demographic information, etc. This can be a very valuable asset to an advertiser.

In another example, the producer of the program, whether it be an on-air program, a program embedded in a video tape, CD-ROM, DVD, or a cassette, can allow the user to automatically access additional information that is not displayed on the screen. For example, in a sporting event, various statistics can be provided to the user from a remote location, merely by the viewer watching the program. When these statistics are provided, the advertiser can be provided with demographic information and background information regarding the user. This can be important when, for example, the user may record a sports program. If the manufacturer sees that this program routing code is being output from some device at a time later than the actual broadcast itself, this allows the advertisers to actually see that their program

is still being used and also what type of individual is using it. Alternatively, the broadcaster could determine the same and actually bill the advertiser an additional sum for a later broadcast. This is all due to the fact that the routing information automatically, through a PC and a network, will provide an indication to the advertiser the time at which the actual information was broadcast.

The different type of medium that can be utilized with the above embodiment are such things as advertisements, which are discussed hereinabove, contests, games, news programs, education, coupon promotional programs, demonstration media (demos), and photographs, all of which can be broadcast on a private site or a public site. This all will provide the ability to allow realtime interface with the network and the remote location for obtaining the routed information and also allow for realtime billing and accounting.

Referring now to FIG. 16, there is illustrated an alternate embodiment of the present disclosure, this being the preferred embodiment. In the embodiment of FIG. 16, as compared to that of FIG. 1, the advertiser does not provide an advertisement in the form of a tone to the broadcast program source 104. Rather, the program source 104, which is remote with respect to the user PC 112, is now replaced with a system which is local to the user PC 112. This local system comprises an audio extractor 1600 which is operable to receive any of a number of analog and digital inputs, for example, which inputs include a video cassette recorder (VCR) 1602 for playing analog tape media having audio/video content thereon, a digital video disk (DVD) unit 1604 for playing DVD disk media having digital audio/video content thereon, a digital audio tape (DAT) unit for playing tape media having digital audio content thereon, and a compact disk (CD) unit 1608 for playing CD media having digital audio content thereon. Note that each of the aforementioned units (1602, 1604, 1606, and 1608) may connect directly to the user PC 112 such that the extraction process using the audio extractor 1600 is performed internal to the user PC 112. Each of the media have audible tones encoded thereon. These audible tones are extracted from the respective signals from one or more of the media by the audio extractor 1600 which may simply perform template matching in order to identify and extract the embedded tone information. The tone is then played through an audio transmitter 1612 (e.g., a speaker). An audio receiver 1614 (e.g., a microphone) connects to the user PC 112 and is operable to receive the audible tones from the audio transmitter 1612. The analog audible signal is then converted to a digital signal by conventional means.

Software running on the user PC 112 responds to the audible tone received through the audio receiver 1614 by detecting and decoding the tone, and launching a communication program (e.g., a web browser program) which is operable to communicate over the network through the modem 114. The software running on the user PC 112 assembles a message packet which contains routing information directed to the ARS 308 and the decoded information of the audible tone. The software running on the user PC 112 via the communication program facilitates the linking of the local node (where the user PC 112 is located) to the ARS 308 (an intermediate node location) and transmits the message packet in accordance with information stored in the program info database 116 through a the modem 114 to the ARS 308 disposed on the network.

It can be appreciated that the audio extractor 1600 is operable to accept any units or systems whose outputs contain audio signals. Furthermore, it can be appreciated

that the audio extractor 1600 is operable to receive analog or digital signals containing audio content from the user PC 112 over a connection 1610. For example, if the user of the user PC 112 desires to download an audio or audio/video file from a remote location on a network (not shown) on which both the remote location and the user PC 112 are disposed, the user may then play the file such that the video portion is displayed on the display 118 while the audio portion including the audible tone is output through the audio extractor 1600 to the audio transmitter 1612 of the user PC 112. An audio receiver 1614 (e.g., a microphone) is operable to receive all audible audio signals, but working in conjunction with onboard architecture, responds only to those embedded audible tones.

Referring now to FIG. 17, there is illustrated an overall diagrammatic view of the interconnection over the network of the user PC 112, it now being referred to as user PC 1702 in FIG. 17. The user PC 1702 is interconnected with the network 306, as described hereinabove with reference to FIG. 3, to allow the user PC 1702 to forward the decoded information of the received audible tone to the ARS 308. As described hereinabove, this forwarding operation is facilitated by a detection operation in the user PC 1702. The user PC 1702 detects the presence of the audible tone received from the audio source 1700. (The audio source 1700 in this illustration comprises any of one or more of the audio sources-VCR 1602, DVD 1604, DAT 1606, and CD 1608.) The user PC 1702 then utilizes this information to connect to the ARS 308, in conjunction with stored information in the user PC 1702, and forwards the received tone or the decoded information contained therein, or even a portion of the information contained therein, to the ARS 308. The ARS 308 utilizes this information for comparison with a relational database 1704 to define or to correlate the received tone information with routing information for a destination node 1706 on the network 306. Once the ARS 308 has determined that there is routing information that correlates to the tone information received from the user PC 1702, then this information is assembled in a packet and transferred back to the user PC 1702. The user PC 1702 then utilizes this redirected routing information to allow the user PC 1702 to make a connection with the destination node 1706. This destination node 1706 can then transmit information back to the user PC 1702 in the form of a web page or the such. As described hereinabove, a web browser software program is utilized to interface with the ARS 308 and the destination node 1706.

As an example, consider the situation where a recording company contracts with a retail outlet store having a web page that resides at the destination node 1706 to control the user PC 1702 at the user location on the network. The recording company embeds a tone in the media to cause the user PC 1702 to connect to the retail outlet store destination node 1706 whenever that audible tone is transmitted from the recording media. For example, the retail outlet may be a video/music store that would desire certain specials or new releases to be relayed to a user at certain times during play of the recording media. The recording company can determine that a particular tone be embedded within an audio or video track on the media that is correlated with the destination node 1706 address of the retailer on the network 306, and then transmit this tone at the appropriate time or at the appropriate point in the program. This need not be a specific time, or it can be a specific time in the program.

Therefore, the recording company can selectively control the user PC 1702 at a user location on the network 306 to connect to a desired destination node 1706 merely by

injecting a tone into the recording media, or any other type of encoded information. This may be perceptible by the user or it may not be perceptible. Further, the embedded information could cause an optical coupling between the user PC **1702** and the audio source **1700**, rather than an audio coupling means using both the audio transmitter **1612** and the audio receiver **1614**. It is only necessary that some code or information be embedded into the recording media and that there be some type of detector at the user's end to detect this information to then effect a connection over the network **306**. The implementation of the ARS **308** allows the recording company to initiate regular updates to the relational database **1704**. The updates may be new audio or video releases which are now linked in the relational database **1704** to the particular tone embedded in the recording media. In this way, the repeated use of the recording media by the user causes new information to be displayed to the user at the user PC **1702**, precluding the recording media from becoming "outdated."

In addition to being able to transmit the encoded information that is detected by the PC **1702** back to the ARS **308** from the user PC **1702**, a user ID in the user PC **1702** can be transmitted to the ARS **308**. The ARS **308** has contained therein a user profile database **1708** which is set up by the user when the software detection program is initially loaded, which user profile is associated with the user ID. This user profile information is optional, but can be utilized by the ARS **308** for multiple purposes. One of these purposes could be that the user profile information is appended to the routing information extracted from the relational database **1704** and forwarded back to the user PC **1702**. When the user PC **1702** and the browser program therein contact the destination node **1706**, the user profile information received from the ARS **308** is appended thereto. Therefore, the destination node **1706** will have information regarding the user that is contacting the destination node **1706**. The flexibility provided by the disclosed architecture is enormous in that the relational database **1704** may be structured to hold any amount of information related to the user such that play of the particular recording media at a particular moment in time triggers display of different information.

Referring now to FIG. **18**, there is illustrated a flowchart depicting the operation at the recording media architecture. The program is initiated at a block **1800** and then proceeds to a function block **1802** where the user inserts and plays the recording media. Flow is then to a function block **1804** where the audio extractor **1600** extracts the embedded tone signal from the audio/video signals of the recording media at the audio/video source **1700**. Flow is then to a function block **1806** where the audio extractor **1600** outputs the tone signal to the audio transmitter **1612**. Flow is then to a function block **1808** where the tone signal is received into the user PC **1702** by coupling the audible tone signal from the audio transmitter **1612** to the audio receiver **1614**. Flow is then to a function block **1810** where software running on the user PC **1702** assembles an intermediate node routing message packet. This intermediate routing message packet includes routing information of the intermediate node, the intermediate node in this particular disclosure being the ARS **308**. Additionally, the intermediate node routing message packet contains the tone signal or product identifier information decoded from the tone signal as extracted from the recording media. Flow is then to a function block **1812** where software running on the user PC **1702** launches a web browser for transmitting the intermediate node routing message packet across the network **306**.

Flow is then to a function block **1814** where the message packet is transmitted to the intermediate node (ARS **308**). Flow is then to a function block **1816** where a matching process occurs wherein the tone signal or decoded product information is obtained from the message packet and matched with corresponding tone signal information residing on the relational database **1704**. Flow is then to a decision block **1818** where the matching process is performed and if a match does not occur, flow is out the "N" path to a function block **1820** where a message is returned to the user indicating that the match was unsuccessful. If a match does occur, flow is out the "Y" path to a function block **1822** where a destination node message packet is assembled with routing information of the destination node corresponding to the tone signal. Flow is then to a function block **1824** where this destination node message packet having routing information of the destination node is transmitted back to the user PC **1702**. Flow is then to a function block **1826** where the user PC **1702** is then redirected to connect to the destination node **1706**. Flow is then to a function block **1828** where the destination node **1706** then returns information for display to the user PC **1702** corresponding to the tone signal information provided in the destination node message packet. Flow is then to an end point **1830** where the program terminates.

In summary, there is provided a method for allowing a user PC to be controlled in order to effect a connection between the user PC and a destination node on a network. This is facilitated through an audio source such as recording media having an embedded audio signal therein. When the recording media is played, the audio signal is extracted by an audio extractor and transmitted to the user PC, and detected by a program running in the background of the user PC. Once the audible tone is detected, a web browser is launched and the tone or decoded product identifier information associated with the tone is transmitted to an ARS on the network. The ARS then compares the information received from the user PC using information from a relational database. The relational database contains routing information for various destination nodes on the network. When a match occurs, the matching information is then forwarded back to the user PC and this is utilized to route the user PC to the particular destination node corresponding to the audible tone for the display of information therefrom.

Although the preferred embodiment has been described in detail, it should be understood that various changes, substitutions and alterations can be made therein without departing from the spirit and scope of the invention as defined by the appended claims.

What is claimed is:

1. A method for controlling a computer with recorded information of a digital video disk to obtain information from a vendor at a vendor location on a network, comprising the steps of;

embedding a unique user perceivable code in digital recorded video information of the digital video disk such that the unique user perceivable code will be output during the normal playback of the digital recorded video information and within the video/audio bandwidth thereof, the unique user perceivable code in close association with vendor routing information defining the route over the network from a user location to the vendor location, wherein the user location further includes user ID information that uniquely identifies the user location;

operating the video disk at the user location disposed on the network to read the digital recorded video infor-

mation therefrom and outputting the read digital recorded video information on a display at the user location;

extracting the unique user perceivable code with an extractor during output of the digital recorded video information to a user at the user location; and

in response to the step of extracting the unique user perceivable code, transmitting the unique user perceivable code and the user ID information from the user location to an intermediate location on the network in accordance with intermediate location routing information stored at the user location;

accessing at the intermediate location a database of vendor routing information in response to receiving at the intermediate location the transmitted unique user perceivable code from the user location, the database providing and association between the unique user perceivable code and a vendor location on the network and includes user profile information which is associated therein with the user ID information of the user location, there being a plurality of such vendor routing information stored in the database;

comparing the received unique user perceivable code with the stored unique user perceivable codes associated with vendor routing information in the database;

if there is a match between the received unique user perceivable code and any of the stored unique user perceivable codes associated with vendor routing information, and the received user ID information of the user location with the stored user profile information associated with the received user ID information, transmitting the vendor routing information corresponding to the matched unique user perceivable codes back to the user location; and

in response to receiving the matching vendor routing information at the user location, interconnecting the user location with the vendor location over the network and receiving vendor information therefrom wherein the vendor routing information and the matching stored profile information is returned to the user location from the intermediate location for processing by a computer at the user location to control the operation thereof to access the information from the vendor at the vendor location on the network, and wherein the stored profile information is sent to the vendor location.

2. The method of claim 1, wherein the network is a global communication network that provides a universal resource locator (URL) for each location on the network and the routing information is comprised of the URL for the location.

3. The method of claim 1, wherein the unique perceivable code is an audible tone that was output within the audio/video bandwidth of playback and it is perceivable.

4. A method for controlling a computer with recorded information of a digital video disk to obtain information from a vendor at a vendor location on a network, comprising the steps of:

embedding a unique user perceivable code in digital recorded video information such that the unique user perceivable code will be output during the normal

playback of the digital recorded video information and within the video/audio bandwidth thereof, the unique user perceivable code in close association with vendor routing information defining the route over the network from a user location to the vendor location, wherein the user location further includes user ID information that uniquely identifies the user location;

operating the video disk at the user location disposed on the network to read the digital recorded video information therefrom and outputting the read digital recorded video information on a display at the user location;

extracting the unique user perceivable code with an extractor during output of the digital recorded video information to a user at the user location;

in response to extracting the unique user perceivable code, transmitting the unique user perceivable code and user ID information from the user location to an intermediate location disposed on the network in accordance with intermediate location routing information of the intermediate location stored at the user location;

performing a matching operation of unique user perceivable codes associated with vendor routing information stored at the intermediate location with the received unique user perceivable code including the steps of:

accessing at the intermediate location a database of vendor routing information in response to receiving at the intermediate location the transmitted unique user perceivable code from the user location, the database providing an association between the unique user perceivable code and the vendor location on the network and user profile information which is associated in with the user ID information of the user location, there being a plurality of such vendor routing information stored in the database, to return to the user location matching vendor routing information of a vendor location disposed on the network and stored profile information matching the received user ID information, the vendor location having the vendor information contained thereat; and

in response to receiving the matching vendor routing information at the user location, interconnecting the user location with the vendor location over the network in accordance with the vendor routing information and receiving the vendor information therefrom and sending the matching stored profile information to the vendor location for processing by a computer at the user location to control the operation thereof.

5. The method of claim 4, wherein the network is a global communication network that provides a universal resource locator (URL) for each location on the network and the routing information is comprised of the URL for the location.

6. The method of claim 4, wherein the unique user perceivable code is an audible tone that was output within the audio/video bandwidth of playback and it is perceivable.

\* \* \* \* \*

## Launching a web site using a passive transponder

**United States 8,028,036**

Issued September 27, 2011

A method of displaying a web page to a user. A triggering device (2502) having a unique code stored therein is provided to the user. The unique code is extracted from the triggering device (2502) with an activation system (302), the activation system (302) disposed on a network (306). Location information associated with the unique code is retrieved from a database (1614 or 310), the location...

## Method and apparatus for utilizing an audibly coded signal to conduct commerce over the internet

**United States 8,005,985**

Issued August 23, 2011

A method and apparatus for utilizing a coded audio/video signal to conduct commerce over the Internet. Broadcast information is broadcast from a remote location on a secondary network containing video over the secondary network to a location thereon proximate the location of the user PC. Unique information is encoded in the broadcast information representative of a location on the primary network...

## Software downloading using a television broadcast channel

**United States 7,996,552**

Issued August 9, 2011

 A software distribution architecture having a television broadcast system as its infrastructure. Software from a software repository (1600) is mixed into a television broadcast system and transmitted into one or more selected channels at prescribed dates and times. An at-home subscriber, capable of receiving with a receiver (1608) the one or more select channels, switches to the one or more...

## Method and apparatus for connecting a user location to one of a plurality of destination locations on a network

**United States 7,979,576**

Issued July 12, 2011

A method for interconnecting a user's location to a destination location on a network. The unique information is received at the user's location, which unique information has no associated routing information embedded therein. Network routing information is associated with the received unique information in response to receipt thereof. The user's location is then interconnected to the...

## Launching a web site using a passive transponder

**United States 7,975,022**

Issued July 5, 2011

A method of displaying a web page to a user. A triggering device having a unique code stored therein is provided to the user. The unique code is extracted from the triggering device with an activation system, the activation system disposed on a network. Location information associated with the unique code is retrieved from a database, the location information corresponding to a location of the...

## Method and apparatus for completing, securing and conducting an E-commerce transaction

**United States 7,930,213**

Issued

A method of conducting and on-line transaction. A user at a PC (302) of a first location completes a profile information sheet and transmits it across a secure network (2708) to a central registration server (2704) at a second location also disposed on the network (306). The central registration server (2704) transmits a unique bar code and associated unique ID back to the user PC (302) at the...

## Method for connecting a wireless device to a remote location on a network

**United States 7,925,780**

Issued April 12, 2011

A method for connecting a wireless device to a remote location on a computer network. A beacon signal is transmitted from a beacon unit to a beacon signal receiver circuit disposed with a wireless device. The beacon signal includes components indicative of a first code associated with a remote location and of a second code associated with an attribute of the beacon unit. A first message packet...

## Input device for allowing input of unique digital code to a user's computer to control access thereof to a web site

**United States 7,912,961**

Issued March 22, 2011

A method for controlling a computer is disclosed wherein one or more remote locations disposed on a network are accessed in response to scanning an optical code. A first computer disposed on the network connects to a scanner for scanning the optical code of a product by a user. The scanner is uniquely identified with a scanner distributor by a scanner identification number. A second computer...

## Method and apparatus for utilizing a unique transaction code to update a magazine subscription over the internet

**United States 7,912,760**

Issued March 22, 2011

A method for completing an electronic commerce transaction over a global communication network initiated between a vendor and a potential consumer. The method includes the steps of associating a unique transaction code with the initiated transaction between the vendor and the potential consumer for use by the consumer in completing a specific electronic commerce transaction; associating user...

## Automatic configuration of equipment software

**United States 7,908,467**

Issued

An architecture for automatically configuring software of a piece of equipment. The piece of equipment is in communication with a network, the piece of equipment having one or more machine-resolvable codes associated therewith. The piece of equipment connects to a remote location disposed on the network in response to reading a select one of the one or more machine-resolvable codes with a reader....

## Accessing a vendor web site using personal account information retrieved from a credit card company web site

**United States 7,904,344**

Issued March 8, 2011

A method of accessing a vendor web site (3422) over a global communication packet-switched network (306) using personal account information of a credit card (3400) retrieved from a credit card company server (3300) on the network (306). At a user location disposed on the network, a machine-resolvable code (MRC) (3402) of the credit card (3400) of a user is read with a reading device (3410). Coded...

## Method and apparatus for utilizing an audible signal to induce a user to select an E-commerce function

**United States 7,900,224**

Issued March 1, 2011

A method for delivering advertising to a consumer over a broadcast media/global communication network combination. An advertisement broadcast is generated comprised of a general program and associated advertising dispersed there through for broadcast over a broadcast media which is directed to a general class of consumers. Unique information is embedded in the broadcast for inducing a consumer to...

## Method and apparatus for accessing a remote location by receiving a product code

**United States 7,886,017**

Issued February 8, 2011

A method for controlling a computer is disclosed wherein one or more remote locations disposed on a network are accessed in response to accessing a product code. A first computer

disposed on the network connects to a device for accessing the product code of a product by a user. The device is uniquely identified with a device distributor by a device identification number. A second computer...

### Input device having positional and scanning capabilities

**United States 7,870,189**

Issued January 11, 2011

A multi-purpose input device (2500) for providing conventional positional tracking, and one or more read capabilities for automatically connecting a user PC (302) to remote node. In one embodiment, a user reads optically encoded indicia (1606) of a product by passing the input device (2500) thereover. A software interface (2505) processes the read information, assembles a message packet, and...

### Method for interfacing scanned product information with a source for the product over a global network

**United States 7,822,829**

Issued October 26, 2010

A method for interfacing scanned product information with a source for the product over a global network. A method is provided for obtaining information regarding the source of a product from a remote information source location on a global communication network utilizing a product code associated with the product and unique thereto. The product code associated with the product is scanned with a...

### Portable scanner for enabling automatic commerce transactions

**United States 7,819,316**

Issued October 26, 2010

A method for initiating and completing a commercial transaction is disclosed that allows a user to acquire and own an article of commerce having associated therewith a machine resolvable code (MRC), the MRC having encoded therein information relating to the article of commerce, the user having unique identification information associated with the user. The MRC is first recognized and a...

### Retrieving personal account information from a web site by reading a credit card

**United States 7,818,423**

Issued October 19, 2010

A method of accessing personal account information of a credit card (3400) over a global communication packet-switched network (306). At a user location disposed on the network (306), a machine-resolvable code (MRC) (3402) of the credit card (3400) of a user is read with a reading device (3410). Coded information is extracted from the MRC (3402). Routing information associated with the coded...

## Method and apparatus for allowing a broadcast to remotely control a computer

**United States 7,792,696**

Issued September 6, 2010

The present invention disclosed and claimed herein comprises a system and method for launching an advertisement on a computer having an audio input interface and a display; an audio output acoustically coupled from a broadcast source to the input interface for outputting an audio signal having encoded therein an advertisement; and a program operable on the computer and responsive to the audio...

## Launching a web site using a personal device

**United States Launching a web site using a personal device**

Issued June 15, 2010

A method of displaying a web page to a user. A triggering device (2500) is provided having a unique code associated therewith, the unique code associated with a remote location on a network of the source of the web page. The unique code is transmitted from the triggering device (2500) to an interface system (302), which interface system (302) is disposed on the network (306) at a triggering...

## Network routing utilizing a product code

**United States 7,694,020**

Issued April 6, 2010

A method for utilizing a product code having product information contained therein for interfacing over a network. A representation of the product information is extracted from the product code, which product code is disposed on or in close association with an associated product. In response to this extraction, network routing information is associated with the product code information.

## Method and apparatus for automatic configuration of equipment
**United States 7,653,446**

Issued January 26, 2010

An architecture for automatically configuring equipment. A piece of equipment connected externally to a user PC has one or more machine-resolvable codes (MRCs) associated therewith. The piece of equipment receives configuration information from a remote location disposed on the network in response to reading a select one of the one or more MRCs with a reader. Configuration information associated...

## Method and apparatus for matching a user's use profile in commerce with a broadcast
**United States 7,636,788**

Issued

A method for advertising over a network and broadcast media combination. A user's computer at a location on the network is operable to receive a signal from a broadcast generated by an advertiser, which signal has embedded therein unique coded information. The user's computer is connected to an advertiser's location in response to extracting a representation of the audio signal...

## Method and apparatus for utilizing an existing product code to issue a match to a predetermined location on a global network

**United States 7,596,786**

Issued September 29, 2009

A method for providing an interconnection relationship between a product and a desired location on a global communications network. A machine readable product code is disposed on the product machine readable product code, the machine readable product code having encoded product information contained therein. The product code has no routing information embedded therein which would allow the...

## Method for configuring a piece of equipment with the use of an associated machine resolvable code

**United States 7,558,838**

Issued July 7, 2009

An architecture for automatically configuring equipment interfaced to a computer. A computer which is in communication with a network, is provided having the piece of equipment interfaced to the computer and having associated therewith one or more machine-resolvable codes (MRCs). The computer connects to a remote location disposed on the network in response to a select one of the one or more MRCs...

## Software downloading using a television broadcast channel

**United States 7,548,988**

Issued June 16, 2009

A software distribution architecture having a television broadcast system as its infrastructure. Software from a software repository (1600) is mixed into a television broadcast system and transmitted into one or more selected channels at prescribed dates and times. An at-home subscriber, capable of receiving with a receiver (1608) the one or more select channels, switches to the one or more...

## Method and apparatus for opening and launching a web browser in response to an audible signal

**United States 7,536,478**

Issued May 19, 2009

The present invention disclosed and claimed herein comprises a system and method for launching a web browser on a network comprising a computer having an all new input interface and a communication interface coupled to a computer network; said audio input coupled to the audio output of a source for receiving an audio signal having encoded therein a unique code that is associated with a...

## Method and apparatus for accessing a remote location with an optical reader having a programmable memory system

**United States 7,533,177**

Issued May 12, 2009

A method of accessing a remote location on a network using an optical reader. The optical reader includes an optical scanning system, a programmable memory system and an output circuit and is user-switchable between a scan mode, a record mode and a playback mode. The optical reader transmits a code to a first computer disposed on the network. When the optical reader is in the scan mode, the code...

## Method for interconnecting two locations over a network in response to using a tool

**United States 7,526,532**

Issued April 28, 2009

A method for accessing information over a network. A tool is utilized in conjunction with an operation on a user's processor at a user location on the network. The tool has associated therewith a unique tool ID. In response to utilizing the tool, the user's location is interconnected on the network to a predetermined destination at a remote location on the network, which destination has...

## Control of software interface with information input to access window

**United States 7,523,161**

Issued April 21, 2009

A method is disclosed for controlling the software interface of a user's computing device to display information on a display in proximity to the physical location of the user's computing device. The interface is operable to display to a user on the display at least one access window that is operable to access information about a product, which access window requires the user to input a...

## Method and apparatus for utilizing a unique transaction code to update a magazine subscription over the internet

**United States 7,505,922**

Issued March 17, 2009

The present invention disclosed herein comprises a method for completing an electronic commerce transaction over a global communication network initiated between a vendor and a

potential consumer. The method includes the steps of associating a unique transaction code with the initiated transaction between the vendor and the potential consumer for use by the consumer in completing a specific...

## Launching a web site using a portable scanner

### United States 7,496,638

Issued February 24, 2009

A method for a user to access information on a network. Information from a machine recognizable code (MRC) (1606) is extracted at a user location, which MRC (1606) has associated therewith routing information to a remote location (312) on the network. The extracted information from the MRC (1606) is wirelessly transmitted to a network interface device (302) in response to the information being...

## Controlling a PC using a tone from a cellular telephone

### United States 7,493,384

Issued February 17, 2009

A method and apparatus for accessing information over a network (306) from a remote location (312) on the network (306) for delivery to a user PC (302). A cellular telephone (2500) is provided having a functional mode for web access over the network (306). A button (2502) on the phone is associated with the functional mode. The button on the phone (2500) is activated by a user to induce the...

## Performing an e-commerce transaction from credit card account information retrieved from a credit card company web site

### United States 7,493,283

Issued February 17, 2009

A method of conducting an e-commerce transaction on a global communication network (306) by using personal account information of a credit card retrieved from a credit card company server on the network (306). At a user location disposed on the network, a machine-resolvable code (MRC) (3402) of the credit card (3400) of a user is read with a reading device (3410). Coded information is extracted...

## Method and apparatus for allowing a remote site to interact with an intermediate database to facilitate access to the remote site

### United States 7,487,259

Issued February 3, 2009

Method and apparatus for allowing a remote site to interact with an intermediate database to facilitate access to the remote site a method for delivering information from a source on a global communication network to destination location thereon. A unique code is associated with an advertising action associated with the source location. The unique code is stored in a database and routing...

**Method and apparatus for launching a web browser in response to scanning of product information**

**United States 7,440,993**

Issued October 21, 2008

A method for interconnecting a user's location to a destination location on a network. The unique information is received at the user's location, which unique information has no associated routing information embedded therein. Network routing information is associated with the received unique information in response to receipt thereof. The user's location is then interconnected to the...

**Method and apparatus for utilizing an audibly coded signal to conduct commerce over the internet**

**United States 7,437,475**

Issued October 14, 2008

A Method and apparatus for utilizing a coded audio/video signal to conduct commerce over the Internet. Broadcast information is broadcast from a remote location on a secondary network containing video over the secondary network to a location thereon proximate the location of the user PC. Unique information is encoded in the broadcast information representative of a location on the primary network...

**Input device for allowing interface to a web site in association with a unique input code**

**United States 7,428,499**

Issued September 23, 2008

An input device for allowing interface to a web site in association with a unique input code. A method for interconnecting a first location on a global communication network with a second location thereon is disclosed. An input device is provided at the first location on the global communication network having associated therewith a unique input device ID. A product code disposed on a product is...

**Method using database for facilitating computer based access to a location on a network after scanning a barcode disposed on a product**

**United States 7,424,521**

Issued September 9, 2008

A visual indicia for facilitating computer based access of a network by consumer. A machine readable code is disposed on a surface having encoded therein information as to a product or a surface, which machine readable code has no routing information contained therein to allow a user to access any location on a network. A visual indicia is disposed on the surface indicative of a relationship...

**Method for interfacing scanned product information with a source for the product over a global network**

**United States 7,415,511**

Issued August 19, 2008

A method for interfacing scanned product information with a source for the product over a global network. A method is provided for obtaining information regarding the source of a product from a remote information source location on a global communication network utilizing a product code associated with the product and unique thereto. The product code associated with the product is scanned with a...

## Method for conducting a contest using a network

### United States 7,412,666

Issued August 12, 2008

A method for conducting a contest using a network is provided. A plurality of pick spaces, a virtual display fixture, and a plurality of virtual articles of commerce are displayed on the screen of a user computer. The user computer is disposed at a user site and operably connected to the network. Initially, the virtual articles of commerce are arrayed on the virtual display fixture. At least one...

## Method and apparatus for controlling a user's pc through a broadcast communication to archive information in the user's pc

### United States 7,398,548

Issued July 8, 2008

A method for allowing a consumer to access an advertiser's location over a global communication network. A normal broadcast program is broadcast to a class of consumers having a unique signal embedded therein, which unique signal embedded therein is associated with a particular advertiser and a predetermined location on the network. Additionally, the unique signal has encoded therein a unique...

## Portable scanner for enabling automatic commerce transactions

### United States 7,392,945

Issued July 1, 2008

A method for initiating and completing a commercial transaction to acquire an article of commerce (2502). The article of commerce (2502) has associated therewith a machine resolvable code (MRC) (2504). The MRC (2504) has encoded therein information relating to the article of commerce (2502). The encoded information in the MRC (2504) is extracted therefrom and unique identification information...

## Method for utilizing visual cue in conjunction with web access

### United States 7,392,312

Issued June 24, 2008

The use of a visual indicia or cue facilitates computer based access of a network by a consumer witnessing a presentation. A visual indicia or cue is provided during the presentation indicative of a relationship between the visual indicia or cue in the presence of a location on a network. This allows this location on the network to be accessed by a computer having an appropriate input device for...

## Method for conducting a contest using a network

### United States 7,392,285

Issued June 24, 2008

A method for conducting a contest using a network is provided. A plurality of pick spaces and a rolling counter are displayed on a screen of a computer operably connected to the network at a user site. The rolling counter constitutes successive ones of a plurality of available characters, each character being displayed for a preselected duration. Each time the user performs a predefined selection...

## Launching a web site using a personal device

### United States 7,386,600

Issued June 10, 2008

A method of displaying a web page to a user. A triggering device (2500) is provided having a unique code associated therewith, the unique code associated with a remote location on a network of the source of the web page. The unique code is transmitted from the triggering device (2500) to an interface system (302), which interface system (302) is disposed on the network (306) at a triggering...

## Method and apparatus for tracking user profile and habits on a global network

### United States 7,383,333

Issued June 3, 2008

A method and apparatus for tracking network activity of a user. A user PC (302) disposed on a network (306) runs tracking software which initially requires registration to a registration server (2500). The registration process is initiated by the user entering user information into the tracking software for transmission to the registration server (2500). In response to registration, the...

## Method and apparatus for accessing a remote location with a reader having a dedicated memory system

### United States 7,383,319

Issued June 3, 2008

A method of accessing a remote location on a network using an optical reader. The optical reader has an optical scanning system and a dedicated address memory system. The optical scanning system, in response to the user scanning an encoded indicia therewith, sends to a first computer disposed on the network a scan code indicative of information encoded in the scanned indicia. The dedicated...

## Accessing a vendor web site using personal account information retrieved from a credit card company web site

### United States 7,379,901

Issued May 27, 2008

A method of accessing a vendor web site (3422) over a global communication packet-switched network (306) using personal account information of a credit card (3400) retrieved from a credit card company server (3300) on the network (306). At a user location disposed on the network, a machine-resolvable code (MRC) (3402) of the credit card (3400) of a user is read with a reading device (3410). Coded...

## Software downloading using a television broadcast channel

**United States 7,370,114**

Issued May 6, 2008

A software distribution architecture having a television broadcast system as its infrastructure. Software from a software repository (1600) is mixed into a television broadcast system and transmitted into one or more selected channels at prescribed dates and times. An at-home subscriber, capable of receiving with a receiver (1608) the one or more select channels, switches to the one or more...

## Presentation of web page content based upon computer video resolution

**United States 7,346,694**

Issued March 18, 2008

An architecture for customizing the amount of web page banner advertising content presented to a user. When a user accesses a server node (102) disposed on a network (104), the user computer (100) provides video resolution information to the server node (102). The server node (102) transmits a web page to the user node (100) which corresponds to the video resolution information of the user node...

## Network routing utilizing a product code

**United States 7,321,941**

Issued January 22, 2008

A method for utilizing a product code having product information contained therein for interfacing over a network. The product information is extracted from the product code, which product code is disposed on or in close association with an associated product. In response to this extraction, network routing information is associated with the product code information

## Method and apparatus for utilizing an audibly coded signal to conduct commerce over the internet

**United States 7,318,106**

Issued January 8, 2008

A Method and apparatus for utilizing an audibly coded signal to conduct commerce over the Internet. Broadcast information is broadcast from a remote location on a secondary network over the secondary network to a location, thereon proximate the location of the user PC on a primary network. Unique information is encoded in the broadcast information representative of a location on the primary...

## Optical reader with ultraviolet wavelength capability

**United States 7,314,173**

Issued January 1, 2008

An optical reader is provided for reading a bar code having ultraviolet-wavelength-responsive properties. The optical reader includes an ultraviolet light source, a photodetector, an optical system and a decoder. The ultraviolet light source generates ultraviolet light having a wavelength shorter than visible light and longer than X-rays for illuminating a target region. The photodetector...

**Method and apparatus for automatic configuration of equipment**

**United States 7,308,483**

Issued December 11, 2007

An architecture for automatically configuring equipment. A piece of equipment connected externally to a user PC has one or more machine-resolvable codes (MRCs) associated therewith. The piece of equipment receives configuration information from a remote location disposed on the network in response to reading a select one of the one or more MRCs with a reader. Configuration information associated...

**Aiming indicia for a bar code and method of use**

**United States 7,296,746**

Issued

An aiming indicia is provided for a bar code comprising a sequence of parallel code bars and intervening code spaces disposed along a longitudinal code axis in accordance with a predefined standard. The aiming indicia comprises a non-encoded graphic element disposed on the longitudinal code axis adjacent the bar code and spaced apart from the nearest code bars by a distance of at least 10 times a...

**Method and apparatus for opening and launching a web browser in response to an audible signal**

**United States 7,287,091**

Issued October 23, 2007

The present invention disclosed and claimed herein comprises a system and method for launching a web browser on a network comprising a computer having an all new input interface and a communication interface coupled to a computer network; said audio input coupled to the audio output of a source for receiving an audio signal having encoded therein a unique code that is associated with a...

**Method and apparatus for matching a user's use profile in commerce with a broadcast**

**United States 7,284,066**

Issued October 16, 2007

A method for advertising over a network and broadcast media combination. A user's computer at a location on the network is operable to receive a signal from a broadcast generated by an advertiser, which signal has embedded therein unique coded information. The user's computer

is connected to an advertiser's location in response to extracting the unique coded information from the audio...

## Bar code scanner and software interface interlock for performing encrypted handshaking and for disabling the scanner or input device in case of handshaking operation failure

**United States 7,257,619**

Issued August 14, 2007

An interlocking architecture for a software interface and a bar code scanner. Upon power-up, a handshaking operation is performed between a scanner (1600) having a scanner processor (2600) and a computer processor (2612) of a computer (302) based upon the code stored in the NV memory (2602) of the scanner (1600) and a unique code associated with the software interface running on the computer...

## Digital ID for selecting web browser and use preferences of a user during use of a web application

**United States 7,257,614**

Issued August 14, 2007

A browser configuration architecture where input of a unique user ID automatically configures those browser applications preselected for auto-configuration from entries of a user preferences sheet. The user preferences sheet (2500) is part of the browser control software (2502) used for storing user preferences associated with one or more browser applications (2506, 2508, and 2510) loaded on a...

## Optical reader and use

**United States 7,240,840**

Issued July 10, 2007

An optical reader is provided for reading a symbol representing information having areas of different light reflectivity. The optical reader comprises a radiant energy source, a photodetector, an optical system and a decoder. The radiant energy source generates a radiant energy for illuminating a target region. The photodetector generates output electrical signals indicative of the radiant energy...

## Automatic configuration of equipment software

**United States 7,237,104**

Issued June 26, 2007

An architecture for automatically configuring software of a piece of equipment. The piece of equipment is in communication with a network, the piece of equipment having one or more machine-resolvable codes associated therewith. The piece of equipment connects to a remote location disposed on the network in response to reading a select one of the one or more machine-resolvable codes with a reader....

## Method and apparatus for directing an existing product code to a remote location

**United States 7,228,282**

Issued June 5, 2007

A method for interfacing a user location on a network to a destination location on the network is disclosed. A bar code having product information contained therein relating to an associated product is first scanned with a scanner, which bar code has no network routing information contained therein. The product information contained within the bar code is then extracted. Routing information over...

## Method and apparatus for accessing a remote location with an optical reader having a dedicated memory system

**United States 7,197,543**

Issued March 27, 2007

A method of accessing a remote location on a network using an optical reader. The optical reader has an optical scanning system and a dedicated address memory system. The optical scanning system, in response to the user scanning an encoded indicia therewith, sends to a first computer disposed on the network a scan code indicative of information encoded in the scanned indicia. The dedicated...

## Method for connecting a wireless device to a remote location on a network

**United States 7,191,247**

Issued March 13, 2007

A method for connecting a wireless device to a remote location on a computer network. A beacon signal is transmitted from a beacon unit disposed at a first geographic location. The beacon signal includes components indicative of a first code and of a second code, the first code being associated with a remote location on a computer network and the second code being associated with an attribute of...

## Method and apparatus for utilizing an existing product code to issue a match to a predetermined location on a global network

**United States 7,159,037**

Issued January 2, 2007

A method for providing an interconnection relationship between a product and a desired location on a global communications network. A machine readable product code is disposed on the product machine readable product code, the machine readable product code having encoded product information contained therein. The product code has no routing information embedded therein which would allow the...

## Method and apparatus for launching a web site with non-standard control input device

**United States 7,117,240**

Issued October 3, 2006

A method for launching a web browser application on a user's computer. A browser application is provided on the user's computer that is launchable in response to predetermined browser inputs being received by the user's computer. A non-browser input is provided that is not a

portion of the set of predetermined browser inputs. This non-browser is correlated to the input to simulate one...

## Battery pack having integral optical reader for wireless communication device

**United States 7,089,291**

Issued August 8, 2006

A battery pack for a wireless communication device comprises a housing, at least one battery disposed within the housing and an optical reader disposed within the housing. The housing is adapted to be removably attachable to a wireless communication device. The housing includes an external shell defining an optical port there through and has an operational power interface and a data interface...

## Method and apparatus for controlling a user's PC through an audio-visual broadcast to archive information in the user's PC

**United States 7,069,582**

Issued June 27, 2006

A method for allowing a consumer to access an advertiser's location over a global communication network. A normal broadcast program is broadcast to a class of consumers having a unique signal embedded therein, which unique signal embedded therein is associated with a particular advertiser and a predetermined location on the network. Additionally, the unique signal has encoded therein a unique...

## Method for controlling a computer using an embedded unique code in the content of CD media

**United States 7,043,536**

Issued April 9, 2006

A method for allowing a user PC (1702) to be controlled in order to effect a connection between the user PC (1702) and a destination node (1706) on a network (306). This is facilitated through an audio source (1700) wherein compact disk recording media has embedded therein an audio signal. When the compact disk recording media is played, the audio signal is extracted by an audio extractor (1600)...

## Method of controlling a computer using an embedded unique code in the content of DVD media

**United States 7,010,577**

Issued March 7, 2006

A method for allowing a user PC to be controlled in order to effect a connection between the user PC and a destination node on a network. This is facilitated through an audio source wherein the content of digital video disk recording media has embedded therein an audio signal. When the recording media is played, the audio signal is extracted by an audio extractor and transmitted to the user PC,...

.

**Method and apparatus for allowing a remote site to interact with an intermediate database to facilitate access to the remote site**

**United States 6,985,962**

Issued January 10, 2006

Method and apparatus for allowing a remote site to interact with an intermediate database to facilitate access to the remote site a method for delivering information from a source on a global communication network to a second and a user location thereon. A unique code is associated with an advertising action associated with the source location. The unique code is stored in a database and routing...

**Input device for allowing input of a unique digital code to a user's computer to control access thereof to a web site**

**United States 6,985,954**

Issued January 10, 2006

An input device for allowing input of a unique digital code to a user's computer to control access thereof to a web site. A method for connecting a user computer at a first location on a network with a second location on the network through use of a coded symbol having contained therein encoded information associated with routing information on the network to the second location thereover is...

**Audible designation for a node on a communication network**

**United States 6,981,059**

Issued December 27, 2005

An audible designation for a node on a communication network A method is provided for allowing any of a plurality of first locations on a global communication network to access a specific and determinable second location on the global communication network. A unique audio signature is defined for the specific and determinable second location on the global communication network, which unique audio...

**Method and apparatus for delivering information from a remote site on a network based on statistical information**

**United States 6,973,438**

Issued December 6, 2006

A method and apparatus are disclosed for delivering information, from a content location on a global communication network (GCN) dynamically selected according to statistical information, to a user location thereon. In a computer database, GCN routing information for each of a plurality of content locations on the GCN are associated with a predefined combination of one of a plurality of...

**Method for conducting a contest using a network**

**United States 6,970,916**

Issued November 29, 2005

A method for conducting a contest using a network is provided. Displayed, on a practical screen of a user computer operably connected to the network at a user site, is a plurality of pick spaces, a virtual television set including a first virtual screen, and a virtual computer including a second virtual screen. The apparent area of the first virtual screen constitutes a first display area of the...

### Method and apparatus for embedding routing information to a remote web site in an audio/video track

**United States 6,970,914**

Issued November 29, 2005

A redirect system is provided which is operable to redirect information over a network 1610. This information is associated with a compressed MP3 audio file which is initially transmitted through the network from a source 1612 to a user PC 1600. The user PC 1600 will then play the information and, upon playing the information, embedded information within the audio file will be detected by an...

### System and apparatus for connecting a wireless device to a remote location on a network

**United States 6,961,555**

Issued November 1, 2005

A system for connecting a wireless device to a remote location on a computer network. The wireless device (2510) includes a processor (2714) and a transmitter/receiver (2716) for sending and receiving radio frequency signals (2516) to provide two-way digital communication between the processor and the computer network (306). The system comprises a beacon unit (2502) and a beacon signal receiver...

### Launching a web site using a portable scanner

**United States 6,877,032**

Issued April 5, 2005

A method for a user to access information on a network. Information from a machine recognizable code (MRC) (1606) is extracted at a user location, which MRC (1606) has associated therewith routing information to a remote location (312) on the network. The extracted information from the MRC (1606) is wirelessly transmitted to a network interface device (302) in response to the information being...

### Input device having positional and scanning capabilities

**United States 6,868,433**

Issued March 15, 2005

A multi-purpose input device (2500) for providing conventional positional tracking, and one or more read capabilities for automatically connecting a user PC (302) to remote node. In one embodiment, a user reads optically encoded indicia (1606) of a product by passing the input device (2500) thereover. A software interface (2505) processes the read information, assembles a message packet, and...

### Optical reader and use

**United States 6,860,424**

Issued March 1, 2005

An optical reader is provided for reading a symbol representing information having areas of different light reflectivity. The optical reader comprises a radiant energy source, a photodetector, an optical system and a decoder. The radiant energy source generates a radiant energy for illuminating a target region. The photodetector generates output electrical signals indicative of the radiant energy...

## Web site access manual of a character string into a software interface

**United States 6,845,388**

Issued January 18, 2005

An architecture for accessing a network server using one or more characters. A user computer (302) disposed on a global communication packet-switched network (306) is operable to communicate with an ARS (308) and a destination server (312) also disclosed on the GCN (306). The user computer (302) runs a software interface which displays a window (2500) to the user via a display (1612). The window...

## Aiming indicia for a bar code and method of use

**United States 6,843,417**

Issued January 18, 2005

An aiming indicia is provided for a bar code comprising a sequence of parallel code bars and intervening code spaces disposed along a longitudinal code axis in accordance with a predefined standard. The aiming indicia comprises a non-encoded graphic element disposed on the longitudinal code axis adjacent the bar code and spaced apart from the nearest code bars by a distance of at least 10 times a...

## Method and apparatus for tracking user profile and habits on a global network

**United States 6,836,799**

Issued December 28, 2004

A method and apparatus for tracking network activity of a user. A user PC (302) disposed on a network (306) runs tracking software which initially requires registration to a registration server (2500). The registration process is initiated by the user entering user information into the tracking software for transmission to the registration server (2500). In response to registration, the...

## Method and apparatus for opening and launching a web browser in response to an audible signal

**United States 6,829,650**

Issued December 7, 2004

The present invention disclosed and claimed herein comprises a system and method for launching a web browser on a network comprising a computer having an all new input interface and a communication interface coupled to a computer network; said audio input coupled to the

audio output of a source for receiving an audio signal having encoded therein a unique code that is associated with a...

## Presentation of web page content based upon computer video resolutions

**United States 6,829,646**

Issued December 7, 2004

An architecture for customizing the amount of web page banner advertising content presented to a user. When a user accesses a server node (102) disposed on a network (104), the user computer (100) provides video resolution information to the server node (102). The server node (102) transmits a web page to the user node (100) which corresponds to the video resolution information of the user node...

## Digital ID for selecting web browser and use preferences of a user during use of a web application

**United States 6,826,592**

Issued November 30, 2004

A browser configuration architecture where input of a unique user ID automatically configures those browser applications preselected for auto-configuration from entries of a user preferences sheet. The user preferences sheet (2500) is part of the browser control software (2502) used for storing user preferences associated with one or more browser applications (2506, 2508, and 2510) loaded on a...

## Method and apparatus for accessing a remote location with an optical reader having a programmable memory system

**United States 6,823,388**

Issued November 23, 2004

A method of accessing a remote location on a network using an optical reader. The optical reader includes an optical scanning system, a programmable memory system and an output circuit and is user-switchable between a scan mode, a record mode and a playback mode. The optical reader transmits a code to a first computer disposed on the network. When the optical reader is in the scan mode, the code...

## Method for interfacing scanned product information with a source for the product over a global network

**United States 6,816,894**

Issued November 9, 2004

A method for interfacing scanned product information with a source for the product over a global network. A method is provided for obtaining information regarding the source of a product from a remote information source location on a global communication network utilizing a product code associated with the product and unique thereto. The product code associated with the product is scanned with a...

## Method for configuring a piece of equipment with the use of an associated machine resolvable code

**United States 6,792,452**

Issued September 14, 2004

An architecture for automatically configuring equipment interfaced to a computer. A computer which is in communication with a network, is provided having the piece of equipment interfaced to the computer and having associated therewith one or more machine-resolvable codes (MRCs). The computer connects to a remote location disposed on the network in response to a select one of the one or more MRCs...

## Method for conducting a contest using a network

**United States 6,791,588**

Issued September 14, 2004

A method for conducting a contest using a network is provided. A plurality of pick spaces, a virtual display fixture, and a plurality of virtual articles of commerce are displayed on the screen of a user computer. The user computer is disposed at a user site and operably connected to the network. Initially, the virtual articles of commerce are arrayed on the virtual display fixture. At least one...

## Optical reader with ultraviolet wavelength capability

**United States 6,758,398**

Issued July 6, 2004

An optical reader is provided for reading a bar code having ultraviolet-wavelength-responsive properties. The optical reader includes an ultraviolet light source, a photodetector, an optical system and a decoder. The ultraviolet light source generates ultraviolet light having a wavelength shorter than visible light and longer than X-rays for illuminating a target region. The photodetector...

## Bar code scanner and software interface interlock for performing encrypted handshaking and for disabling the scanner in case of handshaking operation failure

**United States 6,757,715**

Issued June 29, 2004

An interlocking architecture for a software interface and a bar code scanner. Upon power-up, a handshaking operation is performed between a scanner (1600) having a scanner processor (2600) and a computer processor (2612) of a computer (302) based upon the code stored in the NV memory (2602) of the scanner (1600) and a unique code associated with the software interface running on the computer...

## Method and apparatus for accessing a remote location with an optical reader having a dedicated memory system

**United States 6,754,698**

Issued June 22, 2004

A method of accessing a remote location on a network using an optical reader. The optical reader has an optical scanning system and a dedicated address memory system. The optical scanning system, in response to the user scanning an encoded indicia therewith, sends to a first computer disposed on the network a scan code indicative of information encoded in the scanned indicia. The dedicated...

## Method and apparatus for accessing a remote location by scanning an optical code

### United States 6,745,234

Issued June 1, 2004

A method for controlling a computer is disclosed wherein one or more remote locations disposed on a network are accessed in response to scanning an optical code. A first computer disposed on the network connects to a scanner for scanning the optical code of a product by a user. The scanner is uniquely identified with a scanner distributor by a scanner identification number. A second computer...

## Method and apparatus for configuring configurable equipment with configuration information received from a remote location

### United States 6,725,260

Issued April 20, 2004

An architecture for automatically configuring equipment. A piece of equipment connected externally to a user PC has one or more machine-resolvable codes (MRCs) associated therewith. The piece of equipment receives configuration information from a remote location disposed on the network in response to reading a select one of the one or more MRCs with a reader. Configuration information associated...

## Unique bar code for indicating a link between a product and a remote location on a web network

### United States 6,708,208

Issued March 16, 2004

A unique bar code for indicating a link between a product and a remote location on a web network. The present invention dicsclosed and claimed herein, in one aspect thereof, comprises system for connecting between a first location at a user's site on a network and a second and remote location on a network. A unique ornamental symbol encoded with a plurality of dark and light areas is provided...

## Automatic configuration of equipment software

### United States 6,704,864

Issued March 9, 2004

An architecture for automatically configuring software of a piece of equipment. The piece of equipment is in communication with a network, the piece of equipment having one or more machine-resolvable codes associated therewith. The piece of equipment connects to a remote location disposed on the network in response to reading a select one of the one or more machine-resolvable codes with a reader....

**Method and apparatus for accessing a remote location by sensing a machine-resolvable code**

**United States 6,701,369**

Issued March 2, 2004

A method for controlling a computer wherein one or more remote locations disposed on a network are accessed in response to sensing a machine-resolvable code. A computer disposed on a network is operably connected to an input device for sensing a machine-resolvable code. A software application which includes a software identification code runs on the computer. In response to sensing a...

**Method for interconnecting two locations over a network in response to using a tool**

**United States 6,701,354**

Issued March 2, 2004

A method for accessing information over a network. A tool is utilized in conjunction with an operation on a user's processor at a user location on the network. The tool has associated therewith a unique tool ID. In response to utilizing the tool, the user's location is interconnected on the network to a predetermined destination at a remote location on the network, which destination has...

**Method and apparatus for controlling a user's pc through an audio-visual broadcast to archive information in the users pc**

**United States 6,697,949**

Issued February 24, 2004

A method for allowing a consumer to access an advertiser's location over a global communication network. A normal broadcast program is broadcast to a class of consumers having a unique signal embedded therein, which unique signal embedded therein is associated with a particular advertiser and a predetermined location on the network. Additionally, the unique signal has encoded therein a unique...

**(PT) Método para conectar por meio de interface uma informação escaneada de produto a uma fonte do produto através de uma rede global**

**Mexico PI9913624**

Issued January 15, 2002

(PT) "MéTODO PARA CONECTAR POR MEIO DE INTERFACE UMA INFORMAçãO ESCANEADA DE PRODUTO A UMA FONTE DO PRODUTO ATRAVéS DE UMA REDE GLOBAL". Método para conectar por meio de interface uma informação escaneada de produto com o fabricante do produto através de uma rede global de comunicação (306). Após escanear a informação de...

**PI9913623 -Método para controlar um computador com um sinal de áudio**

**Europe PI9913623**

Issued January 15, 2002

"MéTODO PARA CONTROLAR UM COMPUTADOR COM UM SINAL DE áUDIO". Método para controlar um computador (302) ao se inserir um sinal analógico (111) no computador (302)

para controlar um aplicativo de software navegador de rede. O sinal analógico (111) contém um sinal de acionamento que ativa um software de proprietário, e um identificador de produto. O...

### Remote control having an optical indicia reader

**United States 6,694,356**

Issued February 17, 2004

A method for a user to access information on a network (306). A remote control device (3700) is provided operating in a first and control mode with internally generated control commands and in a second and scanning mode. In the control mode, an appliance at a user location is controlled by wirelessly transmitting the control commands to the appliance. In the scanning mode, a machine recognizable...

### Unique bar code

**United States 6,688,522**

Issued February 10, 2004

A bar code for encoding information in machine-readable form is provided. The bar code comprises a character string including a plurality of characters disposed side-by-side along a longitudinal code axis. Each character is formed by a sequence of code bars and intervening code spaces, the code bars being parallel to one another and to a line defining a bar axis which intersects the code axis....

### Method for controlling a computer using an embedded unique code in the content of video tape media

**United States 6,643,692**

Issued November 4, 2003

A method for allowing a user PC (1702) to be controlled in order to effect a connection between the user PC (1702) and a destination node (1706) on a network (306). This is facilitated through an audio source (1700) wherein the content of a video tape recording media has embedded therein an audio signal. When the video tape media is played, the audio signal is extracted by an audio extractor...

### Method and apparatus for utilizing an audibly coded signal to conduct commerce over the internet

**United States 6,636,896**

Issued October 21, 2003

A method and apparatus for utilizing a coded audio/video signal to conduct commerce over the Internet. Broadcast information is broadcast from a remote location on a secondary network containing video over the secondary network to a location thereon proximate the location of the user PC. Unique information is encoded in the broadcast information representative of a location on the primary network...

### Method for conducting a contest using a network

**United States 6,636,892**

Issued October 21, 2003

A method for conducting a contest using a network is provided. A plurality of pick spaces and a rolling counter are displayed on a screen of a computer operably connected to the network at a user site. The rolling counter constitutes successive ones of a plurality of available characters, each character being displayed for a preselected duration. Each time the user performs a predefined selection...

**Method and system for conducting a contest using a network**

**United States 6,631,404**

Issued October 7, 2003

A method for conducting a contest using a network. A selected article of commerce is identified to a plurality of users remotely disposed at user locations on the network which bears an indicia encoding an identification code which corresponds to the selected article in accordance with an extrinsic standard. An unvalidated entry message packet is then received at a reference location which was...

**Interactive Doll**

**United States 6,629,133**

Issued September 30, 2003

An interactive doll is disclosed having one or more sensors contained therein. The one or more sensors are operable to trigger output of a signal from the doll in response to the one or more sensors being activated by physical stimuli of a user. A processor located with the user and the doll at a first node of a global communication network processes the signal. The processor is operable to link...

**Method and apparatus for allowing a remote site to interact with an intermediate database to facilitate access to the remote site**

**United States 6,622,165**

Issued September 16, 2003

Method and apparatus for allowing a remote site to interact with an intermediate database to facilitate access to the remote site a method for delivering information from a source on a global communication network to a second and a user location thereon. A unique code is associated with an advertising action associated with the source location. The unique code is stored in a database and routing...

**Method for controlling a computer using an embedded unique code in the content of dat media**

**United States 6,615,268**

Issued September 2, 2003

A method for allowing a user PC to be controlled in order to effect a connection between the user PC and a destination node on a network. This is facilitated through an audio source wherein a digital audio tape recording media having embedded therein an audio signal therein.

When the recording media is played, the audio signal is extracted by an audio extractor and transmitted to the user PC, and...

## Method and apparatus for utilizing an audibly coded signal to conduct commerce over the internet

**United States 6,594,705**

Issued July 15, 2003

A Method and apparatus for utilizing an audibly coded signal to conduct commerce over the Internet. Broadcast information is broadcast from a remote location on a secondary network over the secondary network to a location thereon proximate the location of the user PC on a primary network. Unique information is encoded in the broadcast information representative of a location on the primary...

## Method and apparatus for controlling a computer from a remote location

**United States 6,526,449**

Issued February 25, 2003

A method for controlling a user computer is disclosed wherein a broadcast program is operable to transmit a broadcast to the user in the form of an audio/visual program, in addition to an encoded tone. This encoded tone is detected by the user computer and this information then transmitted to an intermediate node, an ARS (308). This tone is compared in a relational database (1704) to determine is...

## Method and system for data transmission from an optical reader

**United States 6,384,744**

Issued May 7, 2002

A method is provided for transmitting data from an optical reader following scanning by the optical reader of an indica encoding information in accordance with one of a plurality of information encoding types. The method includes determining that a particular one of the plurality of encoding types was used for encoding the scanned indicia. A message packet is then transmitted from the optical...

## Routing string indicative of a location of a database on a web associated with a product in commerce

**United States 6,377,986**

Issued April 23, 2002

A method for controlling a computer is disclosed wherein one or more remote locations disposed on a network are accessed in response to scanning an optical code. A first computer disposed on the network connects to a scanner for scanning the optical code of a product by a user. The scanner is uniquely identified with a scanner distributor by a scanner identification number. A second computer...

## Keystroke Automator

**United States D432,539**

Issued October 24, 2000

The ornamental design for keystroke automator, as shown and described.

## Method for controlling a computer with an audio signal

**United States 6,098,106**

Issued August 1, 2000

A method for controlling a computer by inputting an analog signal into the computer to control a web browser software application. The analog signal contains a trigger signal which activates proprietary software, and a product identifier. The proprietary software launches the web browser application on the computer, extracts the product identifier, and creates an appended data string by appending...

## Method of product promotion

**United States 6,928,413**

Issued August 9, 2005

A method of promoting a product. A user at a user location (100) is induced to obtain a first product having a unique ID from a first vendor to win a prize. The user registers the product via a user computer (102) connected on-line to a central registration server (108) across a packet-switched network (104) by completing a user profile and transmitting the user profile and unique ID to a central...

## Método para conectar por meio de interface uma informação escaneada de produto a uma fonte do produto através de uma rede global

**Brazil PI9913624**

Issued January 15, 2002

(PT) "MéTODO PARA CONECTAR POR MEIO DE INTERFACE UMA INFORMAçãO ESCANEADA DE PRODUTO A UMA FONTE DO PRODUTO ATRAVéS DE UMA REDE GLOBAL". Método para conectar por meio de interface uma informação escaneada de produto com o fabricante do produto através de uma rede global de comunicação (306). Após escanear a informação de...

## Método para controlar um computador com um sinal de áudio

**Brazil PI9913623**

Issued January 15, 2002

"MéTODO PARA CONTROLAR UM COMPUTADOR COM UM SINAL DE áUDIO". Método para controlar um computador (302) ao se inserir um sinal analógico (111) no computador (302) para controlar um aplicativo de software navegador de rede. O sinal analógico (111) contém um sinal de acionamento que ativa um software de proprietário, e um identificador de produto. O...

## INDICE DE POINTAGE DESTINE A UN CODE BARRES ET PROCEDE D'UTILISATION

**France PCT/US2001/015970**

Issued June 12, 2001

(FR)L'invention concerne un indice de pointage destiné à un code barres (4000), comportant une séquence de codes barres parallèles (4012) et d'espaces de code (4014) intercalés disposés le long d'un axe de code longitudinal (4010) selon un standard prédéfini. Ledit indice (4050) de pointage comporte un élément graphique (4052) non...

## LECTEUR OPTIQUE ET UTILISATION CORRESPONDANTE
### France WO/2001/093184
Issued December 6, 2001

L'invention concerne un lecteur optique permettant de lire un symbole qui représente une information dotée de zones de réflectivité de lumière différente. Le lecteur optique comporte une source d'énergie radiante, un photodétecteur, un système optique et un décodeur. Ladite source génère une énergie radiante permettant...

## CODE BARRES UNIQUE
### France WO/2001/093187
Issued December 6, 2001

L'invention concerne un code barres destiné à coder des informations sous forme lisible par machine. Ce code barres comporte une chaîne de caractères contenant une pluralité de caractères disposés l'un à côté de l'autre le long d'un axe de code longitudinal. Chaque caractère est formé par une séquence de codes barres...

## Input device for allowing interface to a web site in association with a unique input code
### United States 8,069,098
Issued November 29, 2011

An input device for allowing interface to a web site in association with a unique input code. A method for interconnecting a first location on a global communication network with a second location thereon is disclosed. An input device is provided at the first location on the global communication network having associated therewith a unique input device ID. A product code disposed on a product is...

## (FR) INDICE DE POINTAGE DESTINE A UN CODE BARRES ET PROCEDE D'UTILISATION
### Europe WO/2001/093190
Issued

(FR)L'invention concerne un indice de pointage destiné à un code barres (4000), comportant une séquence de codes barres parallèles (4012) et d'espaces de code (4014) intercalés disposés le long d'un axe de code longitudinal (4010) selon un standard prédéfini. Ledit indice (4050) de pointage comporte un élément graphique (4052) non...

## (FR) INDICE DE POINTAGE DESTINE A UN CODE BARRES ET PROCEDE D'UTILISATION
### Europe WO/2001/093190
Issued June 12, 2001

FR)L'invention concerne un indice de pointage destiné à un code barres (4000), comportant une séquence de codes barres parallèles (4012) et d'espaces de code (4014) intercalés disposés le

long d'un axe de code longitudinal (4010) selon un standard prédéfini. Ledit indice (4050) de pointage comporte un élément graphique (4052) non...

**Method and apparatus for accessing a remote location by sensing a machine-resolvable code**

**United States 8,484,362**

Issued July 9, 2013

A method for controlling a computer wherein one or more remote locations disposed on a network are accessed in response to sensing a machine-resolvable code. A computer disposed on a network is operably connected to an input device for sensing a machine-resolvable code. A software application which includes a software identification code runs on the computer. In response to sensing a...

2 inventors:

- **Hutton (Jovan) Pulitzer**
  Founder FevrTech.org, Flip.Ventures, Xplrr.org and Publisher at InvestigatingHistory.org

- **J Jovan Philyaw**

**Method and apparatus for accessing a remote location with an optical reader having a programmable memory system**

**United States 8,296,440**

Issued October 23, 2012

An optical reader for accessing a remote location on a network includes an optical scanning system, a memory system, an output circuit for interfacing to a first computer disposed on the network, and a switching device for switching between a scan mode, a record mode and a playback mode. The optical reader further includes a transmitter for transmitting code information representative of a code...

3 inventors:

- **Hutton (Jovan) Pulitzer**
  Founder FevrTech.org, Flip.Ventures, Xplrr.org and Publisher at InvestigatingHistory.org

- **j hutton pulitzer**

- **Doug Davis**
  EVP Technology at West Corporation

**Input device for allowing interface to a web site in association with a unique input code**

**United States 8,069,098**

Issued November 29, 2011

An input device for allowing interface to a web site in association with a unique input code. A method for interconnecting a first location on a global communication network with a second location thereon is disclosed. An input device is provided at the first location on the global communication network having associated therewith a unique input device ID. A product code disposed on a product is...

  2 inventors:

- **Hutton (Jovan) Pulitzer**
  Founder FevrTech.org, Flip.Ventures, Xplrr.org and Publisher at InvestigatingHistory.org

- **J Jovan Philyaw**

**Method and apparatus for accessing a remote location by sensing a machine-resolvable code**

**United States 8,484,362**

Issued July 9, 2013

A method for controlling a computer wherein one or more remote locations disposed on a network are accessed in response to sensing a machine-resolvable code. A computer disposed on a network is operably connected to an input device for sensing a machine-resolvable code. A software application which includes a software identification code runs on the computer. In response to sensing a...

**Method and apparatus for accessing a remote location with an optical reader having a programmable memory system**

**United States 8,296,440**

Issued September 23, 2012

An optical reader for accessing a remote location on a network includes an optical scanning system, a memory system, an output circuit for interfacing to a first computer disposed on the network, and a switching device for switching between a scan mode, a record mode and a playback mode. The optical reader further includes a transmitter for transmitting code information representative of a code...

**(EN) AUTOMATIC CONFIGURATION OF EQUIPMENT AND SOFTWARE (FR) CONFIGURATION AUTOMATIQUE D'EQUIPEMENT ET DE LOGICIEL**

**Europe WO/2001/086435**

Issued October 5, 2001

(EN)An architecture for automatically configuring equipment. A piece of equipment connected externally to a user PC has one or more machine-resolvable codes (MRCs) associated therewith.

The piece of equipment receives configuration information from a remote location disposed on the network in response to reading a select one of the one or more MRCs with a reader. Configuration information...

**Method and apparatus for accessing a remote location by sensing a machine-resolvable code**

**United States 8,484,362**

Issued July 9, 2013

A method for controlling a computer wherein one or more remote locations disposed on a network are accessed in response to sensing a machine-resolvable code. A computer disposed on a network is operably connected to an input device for sensing a machine-resolvable code. A software application which includes a software identification code runs on the computer. In response to sensing a...

  2 inventors:

- **Hutton (Jovan) Pulitzer**
  Founder FevrTech.org, Flip.Ventures, Xplrr.org and Publisher at InvestigatingHistory.org


- **jeffry jovan philyaw**

**Method for controlling a computer using an embedded unique code in the content of recorded media**

**United States 8,655,972**

Issued February 18, 2014

A method for controlling a computer with recorded information of a recorded media includes embedding a unique code, which unique code does not contain routing information, in recorded information of the recorded media. The unique code is in close association with vendor information, such that the unique code will be output during normal playback of the information on the recorded media. The...

  2 inventors:

- **Hutton (Jovan) Pulitzer**
  Founder FevrTech.org, Flip.Ventures, Xplrr.org and Publisher at InvestigatingHistory.org


- **jeffry jovan philyaw**

**Method and apparatus for linking a web browser link to a promotional offer**

**United States 8,712,835**

Issued April 29, 2014

A method for offering a promotion to a user. A stimulus is received from a broadcast directed to a user location, the stimulus having unique coded information encoded therein. The unique coded information is extracted from the stimulus by decoding this information. From the decoded information, there is determined routing information for routing over a network to a promotion location on the...

2 inventors:

- **Hutton (Jovan) Pulitzer**
  Founder FevrTech.org, Flip.Ventures, Xplrr.org and Publisher at InvestigatingHistory.org

- **jeffry jovan philyaw**

## Method and apparatus for accessing a remote location with an optical reader having a programmable memory system

### United States 8,296,440
Issued October 23, 2012

An optical reader for accessing a remote location on a network includes an optical scanning system, a memory system, an output circuit for interfacing to a first computer disposed on the network, and a switching device for switching between a scan mode, a record mode and a playback mode. The optical reader further includes a transmitter for transmitting code information representative of a code...

2 inventors:

- **Hutton (Jovan) Pulitzer**
  Founder FevrTech.org, Flip.Ventures, Xplrr.org and Publisher at InvestigatingHistory.org

- **Jeffry Jovan Philyaw**

## Method and apparatus for accessing a remote location by sensing a machine-resolvable code

### United States 8,484,362
Issued July 9, 2013

A method for controlling a computer wherein one or more remote locations disposed on a network are accessed in response to sensing a machine-resolvable code. A computer disposed on a network is operably connected to an input device for sensing a machine-resolvable code. A software application which includes a software identification code runs on the computer. In response to sensing a...